3

The Pre-Grouping Railway Scene - No 1

GREAT WESTERN

Edited by **O. S. NOCK**
BSc, CEng, FICE, FIMechE

LONDON

IAN ALLAN LTD

Contents

First published 1975

ISBN 0 7110 0586 9—126/74

© O. S. Nock, 1975

Published by Ian Allan Ltd, Shepperton, Surrey
and printed and bound in the United Kingdom by
R. J. Acford Ltd, Chichester, Sussex

Preface

From a very early date' in its history the steam locomotive has exercised a remarkable attraction, as much to the photographer and to the scientifically-minded onlooker, as to professional engineers. It is fortunate that this should have been so, and that photographers highly skilled in the use of the primitive apparatus and material then available, should have devoted much time to the locomotives of the day. The work of Bleasdale, Forbes, and the various workers whose results became known to the railway world as 'F. Moore' was outstanding, while at a slightly later period the art of photographing trains in motion was developed by Dr. T. F. Budden, F. E. Mackay, R. J. Purves, and H. Gordon Tidey.

Among those who collected locomotive and train photographs of the pre-grouping period in Great Britain, and set about a most systematic arrangement of their collections, there has surely not been one more devoted, nor more successful than Rixon Bucknall, who was gripped by this particular fancy no less than 60 years ago. Today his massive albums—in some cases two or more covering a single company—form a most comprehensive pictorial record of British locomotive history, and the present book is the first of a series in which a selection has been made of representative pictures from this vast collection, and which it is intended shall eventually comprise the majority of the pre-grouping railway companies of Great Britain.

In the first of these books, dealing with the standard gauge locomotives and trains of the Great Western Railway, a short commentary is given upon each of the pictures. This is a pattern that will be followed in each subsequent volume.

Silver Cedars,   O. S. NOCK
High Bannerdown,   March 1975
Bathcaston, Bath.

Below: A 2–2–2 from the Shrewsbury and Chester Railway, built 1848 by Sharp Bros. and having 5 ft. diameter driving wheels and cylinders 15 in. diameter by 20 in. stroke. In this picture, taken at Wolverhampton, the engine has acquired one of George Armstrong's rolled-top chimney caps. It was preserved at Wolverhampton for many years after withdrawal from service.

Bottom: A 2–2–2 from the West Midland Railway, one of a class of six purchased from Beyer Peacock & Co. just after the formation of the railway in 1861. They had 6 ft. 6 in. driving wheels and 16 in. by 20 in. cylinders. Having inside bearings to the driving axles they could also be described as of the " Jenny Lind " type.

Part One

Wolverhampton – North and West

In a broad generalisation it could be claimed that Wolverhampton was the starting point of the standard gauge network of the GWR. It is certainly difficult to picture the situation that existed there before the vital year of 1854. To appreciate how the Great Western became possessed of an extraordinarily variegated collection of locomotives and rolling stock, eventually based upon Wolverhampton, brief reference must be made to the ruthless and exciting game of railway politics played between the Great Western and its arch-rival then, the London & North Western, in the year between the end of the Gauge War, in 1847, and the amalgamation of the Great Western and the West Midland in 1861.

The report of the Gauge Commissioners had been so watered down by Parliament that the Great Western was not absolutely prohibited from extending the broad gauge network, but every proposal was bitterly opposed—none more so than the Oxford and Birmingham line. The North Western succeeded in getting a clause inserted in the authorising Act that compelled the Great Western to lay it with the " mixed " gauge, and provided the North Western with running powers over it. The latter company never seems to have had the slightest intention of using those powers, any more than the Great Western had of running any standard gauge trains! It was the price that had to be paid for getting the broad gauge into Birmingham. This line was completed in 1852. In the meantime, two small companies farther north had been watching events with some interest.

These were the Shrewsbury & Birmingham and the Shrewsbury & Chester— both standard gauge. Their only outlet to the south had hitherto been over the LNWR; in the traditional manner of those times things had been made so awkward for them that their continued independent existence seemed doubtful, and their eventual absorption by the LNWR only a matter of time.

Both therefore saw a ray of hope in the construction of the *mixed* gauge line from Oxford to Birmingham, and in 1850–1 discussions about co-operation took place between the two Shrewsbury companies and the Great Western. And in the end the very factor inserted as an embarrassment into the technical build-up of the Oxford and Birmingham line, the mixed gauge, led to the two Shrewsbury companies evading LNWR takeover intentions, and their admission into the Great Western fold. That the " powers which were " at Paddington saw in the acquisition of these two small companies a chance of extending the broad gauge to the Mersey is another matter. The physical link-up at Wolverhampton came in the same year, 1854, when the standard gauge Oxford, Worcester & Wolverhampton came in from the south, and the extension of the mixed gauge Great Western from Birmingham joined the OW & W at Priestfield Junction. The OW & W was required to lay in mixed-gauge tracks between the latter point and Wolverhampton, a distance of 2.1 miles. But the entry of the broad gauge into Wolverhampton was no more than a hollow triumph;

for while the Gauge Act of 1846 had provided the tools it was the confrontation at Wolverhampton dating from 1854 that put the first really substantial nail into the coffin of the broad gauge.

Having acquired two very useful little feeder lines in the north they found themselves with no through communication to the rest of the system. It is true that standard gauge rails existed as far south as Oxford, but not beyond; and in any case the GWR had no locomotives or other rolling stock that could work over the line. In this respect, therefore, the take-over was an embarrassment, with all the break-of-gauge inconveniences at Wolverhampton. But included in the take-over was one absolute trump card in the person of Joseph Armstrong, Locomotive Superintendent of the Shrewsbury & Chester Railway. This line, and the Shrewsbury & Birmingham were operated as a single railway, under a joint committee, and in 1853 Armstrong had moved from Chester to Wolverhampton to take charge of the combined locomotive stock. After the amalgamation with the GWR in 1854, a new Northern Division was established covering all lines north of Oxford. Joseph Armstrong was appointed to take charge of all locomotives and their running, reporting of course to Daniel Gooch at Swindon. It did not take Gooch long to appreciate that he had acquired an outstanding lieutenant, and accordingly he gave him a pretty free hand.

To the consternation of all the older Great Western men it soon seemed apparent that the newly-acquired standard gauge " tail " in the north was wagging the broad gauge " dog ", for to facilitate through running the mixed gauge was carried south from Oxford through Didcot and Reading West Junction to the " Hants " fork of the " Berks and Hants " line in order to connect up with the London & South Western at Basingstoke, in 1856, and then to run through from Reading to Paddington by 1861. Nevertheless, if the carrying of mixed-gauge tracks into Paddington was considered sacrilege, it was nothing to the sentiments voiced in Swindon Works,

when they were instructed to build locomotives for the standard gauge! Gooch certainly moved quickly, and by 1856, when the standard gauge link-up with the LSWR was made, he had 12 Swindon-built 0–6–0 goods engines at work and the eight handsome 2–2–2s of the 69 class, which had been built by Beyer, Peacock & Co. These 20 engines were pure Swindon in all but the gauge. Having given Armstrong this starting boost, and followed it with 12 more powerful 0–6–0 goods engines from Swindon, Gooch left him, more or less, to carry on. Two years later Armstrong was designing his own engines for the standard gauge.

It was in this way that the marked individuality of locomotives built or rebuilt at Wolverhampton arose in the first place; and to the miscellaneous collection inherited from the absorbed companies and the first standard-gauge engines designed by Gooch there were gradually added the products of the Armstrong " school ", first of Joseph himself, and then of his mighty brother George, who succeeded him at Wolverhampton when Joseph was chosen to become Locomotive Superintendent of the entire GWR at Swindon in 1864. Before then, however, the equally miscellaneous stock of the West Midland Railway had been added to the existing GWR standard-gauge stud. Altogether it can be said that the only thing that was " standard " about these 300 locomotives was the gauge! With the strong individuality of the Armstrong brothers continuing for another 30 years the variations were not only between Swindon and Wolverhampton, but between the products of brother and brother.

The first dozen or so of the pictures in this album show vividly, at no more than a first glance, the extraordinary variety in outward appearance of the early narrow-gauge locomotive stock, without beginning to enquire into the details of their construction. These locomotives had originated in numerous diverse ways as the standard products of firms like Beyer Peacock, E. B. Wilson, Sharp Stewart, and Fairbairns; in repairing them, and absorbing them into the Wolver-hampton stud, many of the original character-istics were retained, such as the fluted domes of Wilson, the twin-edged brass splashers of Beyer Peacock, and Sharp's highly distinc-tive square-based dome. To these Joseph Armstrong added his own shape of safety-valve column, the like of which was not seen anywhere else, and George Armstrong's rolled top chimneys seemed in direct opposition to the more conventional shape used at Swindon.

Of course the variety of locomotives coming within the area of the Northern Division and maintained from Wolverhampton had been greatly increased after 1861, in which year the West Midland Railway had been absor-bed. This latter line was then a fairly recent example of railway amalgamation, having been made up of the Newport, Abergavenny & Hereford, and the celebrated Oxford, Worcester & Wolverhampton, together with some smaller concerns. Early days on the OW & W—the "Old Worse and Worse" as its nickname had it, had been immorta-lised for locomotive men in the diaries of David Joy, who was running superintendent for some years. It had a pretty shaky set of locomotives when Joy first got there; but one gathers he enjoyed every minute of it, break-downs included! The West Midland and its constituents had always been a purely stan-dard-gauge line, though in pre-constructional days a substantial Great Western investment in it was hoped to secure its allegiance to the broad-gauge fold. Business relations in those early days did not, however, go according to plan, and at one time it was feared that its friendly northern connections at Wolver-hampton might lead to an alliance with the London & North Western instead.

Looking through any collection of 19th century GWR locomotive photographs one is always struck by the remarkable variety of the 2–4–0 tender engines, and in George Arm-strong's time there were plenty of these to be seen at Wolverhampton, and to the north and west of it. The situation was complicated from 1888 onwards, after the completion of the Severn Tunnel, when the Great Western

decided to put on a new express passenger service between Bristol and Shrewsbury. At its northern end this service continued, with through carriages to both the LNWR line, via Crewe, and up the north main line of the GWR to Birkenhead. There were insufficient engines in the Northern Division to power the whole of this new service, and so the working was divided between Bristol and Shrewsbury sheds. The former used 2–4–0s that were typical of "standard-gauge" Swindon of the "1880s" while George Armstrong sent the four rebuilt 2–4–0s of the "Chancellor" class to Shrewsbury, to perform his share of the working. As rebuilt at Wolverhampton in 1878–83 they were a rare mixture of styles, with outside sandwich frames, typical Wolver-hampton boilers and mountings, and cabs having a side-profile unique on the GWR.

Of other 2–4–0 passenger engines working in the Northern Division, which from 1861 included the whole of the former West Mid-land Railway, the variety was such as to delight the photographer and baffle the historian. Some engines in regular service towards the end of the 19th century had begun life as 2–2–2s, and been rebuilt. For-tunately there was not much in the way of renumbering and the earlier pedigrees of some that would otherwise have been mys-teries could eventually be traced. In loco-motives built or rebuilt at Wolverhampton George Armstrong used domed boilers, with the dome on the middle ring of a three-ring barrel, and throughout his time the brass domes and safety valve columns were always lovingly polished, whether the engine was in passenger, goods, or local shunting service.

When Joseph Armstrong went to Swindon in 1864 to become the first Locomotive, Car-riage and Wagon Superintendent of the GWR his brother George had succeeded him at Wolverhampton, and had as his second-in-command and manager at Stafford Road Works, William Dean. But this set-up proved to be short-lived. At Swindon Joseph Arm-strong duly took stock of the existing staff. He came to the conclusion that there was no one there who measured up to Dean for all-round ability, or had the same promise of becoming an eventual head of the locomotive department. So in 1868, to his brother George's surprise and annoyance, Joseph Armstrong transferred Dean to Swindon, and made him Chief Assistant. This made it practically certain that Dean would succeed to the chieftainship, and would step ahead of his former boss at Wolverhampton. Nevertheless Joseph Armstrong had undoubtedly in mind the fact that his brother was only six years younger than himself, and that the line of succession at Swindon called for a man with a longer expectancy of life. Both Joseph Armstrong and Dean knew enough of George's character, of his engineering ability and devotion to the job to leave him to carry on independently at Wolverhampton until 1897, when he was 75 years of age. Of his independence it is enough to recall one fiery retort of his when it was once suggested that some point that had arisen might have to be referred to Swindon. He roared out that " he didn't care a damn for any man and was taking orders from none ". He only *gave* orders, he shouted!

After his brother had gone to Swindon George Armstrong brought out his own design of 2–4–0 express locomotive, and as the photograph on page   shows it was an interesting mixture of external styling. It had a highly ornamental copper-capped chimney and a rather small dome cover, which was painted over. This was the standard practice of the OW & W, which was perpetuated in some of the later GWR locomotives stationed at Worcester. Also he used his brother's style of safety-valve cover. This distinctly individual first essay into locomotive designing became modified into what afterwards was recognised as the true Wolverhampton style, which is very well exemplified in the photograph of one of the same class of locomotives, the 111 class, as rebuilt, No. 1010, standing at the north end of Birmingham Snow Hill station. The style of the 111 class in its later condition was followed by the 3226 class, built at Wolverhampton in 1889, which was sufficiently modern to receive new boilers

with Belpaire fireboxes. The actual locomotive that gave the class its name, No. 111, survived long enough to be photographed buffer to buffer with Churchward's gigantic No. 111 of 1908, *The Great Bear* (see page   ).

But George Armstrong's principal constructional work in the 33 years during which he was undisputed " King of the GWR " at Wolverhampton, was in the production of 0–6–0 shunting and branch-line tank engines. This may, at first thought, seem no more than a humdrum activity; but when it is recalled that at the time of grouping, in 1923, more than one-third of the entire locomotive stock of the GWR, before the additions from the Welsh railways were taken into account, consisted of 0–6–0 tank engines, it will be appreciated that the build-up from Wolverhampton in the latter part of the 19th century was a very important one. Between 1864 and George Armstrong's retirement in 1897 a total of 366 tank engines of the 0–6–0 type was built new at Wolverhampton, and construction of his last standard design continued until 1905, adding another 80 to the stock. Nearly all these engines were originally built as saddle-tanks, but a handsome early example, dating from 1881, was produced by rebuilding some of Daniel Gooch's original standard gauge 0–6–0s. But these followed the wholly indigenous Wolverhampton 1056 class of 1871, which is also illustrated, in a photograph which shows the painted-over dome cover favoured at Worcester. A great number of the Wolverhampton 0–6–0 saddle tanks were afterwards modified to pannier tanks, as exemplified by the illustration of No. 2012 —a George Armstrong engine of 1894.

While with one exception, to be mentioned later, all the Wolverhampton 0–6–0s were of the saddle-tank type, Swindon built a number of 0–6–0s with side tanks. One cannot draw a strict line of demarcation between the products of one works and the other, any more than it is possible to separate their preferences for inside, or outside frames. From 1872 Wolverhampton built naught but inside-framed 0–6–0 saddle tanks, only including outside frames when rebuilds of other engines

8

were concerned. Swindon on the other hand seemed to favour outside frames, down to the year 1887, except when they were building to a standard Wolverhampton design as from 1883 onwards. The Wolverhampton 0–6–0 side tanks previously mentioned were 12 in number, Nos. 633–644, and dated from 1871. They were interesting in having inside frames. In 1902–3, when additional locomotives were needed for the goods traffic on the Metropolitan line to and from Smithfield Market, Churchward took these 30-year-old engines and fitted them with condensing gear for working through the tunnels of the Inner Circle. A further 30 years on it was reported that 10 out of the original 12 were still in service.

The absorption of the West Midland Railway into the GWR together with the extension of mixed-gauge tracks eastwards to London brought some interesting passenger locomotive workings into the Northern Division. The OW & W had always been considered as a main line, and a through passenger train service was developed between Wolverhampton and London, via Worcester. This, no less than the direct London runs via Birmingham and Banbury became a prestige job for the Wolverhampton express drivers, worked entirely by 2–2–2 singles until the very last years of the 19th century. These were all Swindon-built engines, though in maintaining and in certain cases rebuilding them, Wolverhampton succeeded in impressing its own individuality upon them—in one technical matter to their great advantage. I must not dwell upon the origins of these exceedingly pretty little engines at this stage, because none of them were exclusively Northern Division units. This was not because Wolverhampton refrained from building any new 2–2–2 express locomotives.

There was the interesting case of the eight original 2–2–2s of Gooch's design built by Beyer, Peacock in 1855–6. In 1872 George Armstrong set about the modernisation of these engines, and included so much that was new that they became what we should now call an " accountants' rebuild ". There cannot have been much that remained, except the old sandwich frames. Be that as it may, Wolverhampton produced a locomotive of which Ahrons once wrote: " I can truly state as a result of many miles of actual experience on them that they were *for their size* about the best single-driver express engines that ever ran on rails." With his practical training at Swindon, and the many thousands of miles on the footplate that it involved, he was in a good position to judge. It would seem that those in higher authority backed his opinion, because Swindon succeeded in spiriting them away from the Northern Division, and had them at headquarters, and used them on the South Wales trains, working as far west as Neath, and eastwards to Paddington. The South Wales trains then ran via Gloucester, and had to negotiate the heavy gradients leading up to Sapperton Tunnel in the Cotswolds, so that there was very likely a significance in the choice of these Wolverhampton-built 2–2–2s for the job. Whether they remained at Swindon, or whether they were returned to Wolverhampton when the time came for heavy repairs I do not know, but they certainly remained on the South Wales trains until 1887.

This query over the place of their repair concerns the vital matter of valve setting. On a reciprocating steam locomotive, with one of the standard forms of valve gear, the valve setting is fundamentally a matter of compromise. The angularity of the connecting rod imposes a difference between the valve setting for the forward and backward stroke of the piston, and it was in deciding which of the two most obvious compromises in setting to adopt that the practice of Swindon and Wolverhampton differed. One could set for equal " lead " of the valves at each end of the stroke—the lead being the amount the admission valve is open *before* the piston reaches the end of its backward stroke; or one could set for equal port openings. Both were ideals to be aimed at, but with the Stephenson link motion, and equally with the Walschaerts radial gear one could not have both. Swindon set for equal leads; Wolverhampton set for

9

equal port openings. Which was the better? It was definitely a question of running conditions. Lead is important at high speed in providing some cushioning at the end of the piston stroke, and it was naturally desirable, for a smooth-running locomotive, to have this equal at high speed. Because the express locomotive workings with which Swindon was mainly concerned in the latter part of the 19th century mostly involved fairly long non-stop runs over easy gradients the equal-lead setting was a natural choice.

At Wolverhampton things were quite different. The Northern Division has to contend with many more frequent station stops; there were plenty of stiff gradients, against which trains had to be accelerated from rest. A smooth riding engine at high speed was a small consideration against one that could exert a strong, even pull when climbing a bank, or getting smartly away from a station. It was therefore somewhat natural that Wolverhampton adopted the equal port openings technique. They did this, not only on their own purely local engines, and express units like the "Chancellor" class 2-4-0s, but also on the Swindon-built 2-2-2s used on the London expresses. This gave an experienced observer like E. L. Ahrons the opportunity of comparing—from the footplate—the performance of locomotives of the same basic design, but some with the Swindon and others with the Wolverhampton setting. The London-based engines, which shared the workings, had the Swindon setting. His verdict was that the Wolverhampton engines were not only stronger on a bank, but also aster runners. All this was of course a feather in the cap of Wolverhampton.

It was of course a situation that could not last indefinitely. The number of men who combined such immense strength of character as George Armstrong, with great mechanical engineering ability, were few and far between; and it was perhaps just as well that there was no comparable successor in 1897, when Armstrong retired. A situation that could be tolerated on the GWR in the days of William Dean, as a sequel to the earlier set-up at Wolverhampton, would not have been to the liking of a man such as Churchward, and from the beginning of the 20th century Wolverhampton became no more than a divisional station of the locomotive, carriage and wagon department, albeit perhaps the most important after Swindon itself.

A curious 2-2-2 from the Shrewsbury & Hereford Railway, one of six built by the Vulcan Foundry in 1853-4. They had outside framing of a somewhat flimsy construction, with the Stephenson link motion and the valve chests also outside. The cylinders were 15 in. by 20 in. and the driving wheels 5 ft. 6 in. diameter. When this railway became a joint concern of the GWR and the LNWR in 1862, these little 2-2-2s became Great Western property.

Below: In 1860 two fine 0–6–0 goods engines of Matthew Kirtley's design, and built at Derby, were purchased from the Midland Railway. They did well on the Newport, Abergavenny & Hereford section, and in 1861, when Fairbairns were building a further batch for the Midland to exactly the same design the West Midland arranged to have another twelve. It is one of these that is illustrated, and by the time the photograph was taken this had also acquired a "Wolverhampton" chimney top. They were powerful engines with 16 in. by 24 in. cylinders, 5 ft. 2 in. coupled wheels and a boiler pressure of 140 lb. per sq. in.

Bottom: An 0–4–2 from the Birkenhead Railway, about which there is some mystery. It is one of three built by B. Hick & Son, of Bolton, and recorded at Swindon as 2–2–2s at the time of the take-over in 1860. But by the time they were scrapped, in 1863, they had become 0–4–2s.

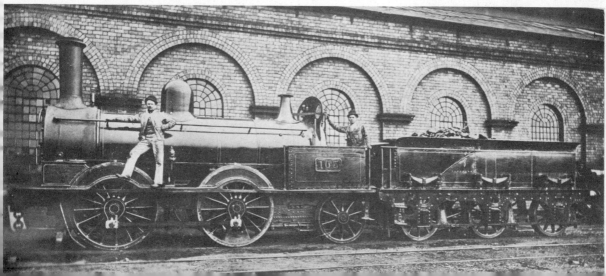

Left: A characteristic Wolverhampton product of the mid-1870s, this neat 0–4–2 tank shows evidence of the changing style of George Armstrong, still keeping the " Beyer " type of chimney, but a " Midland " type of safety-valve column, and the painted-over dome favoured at Worcester.

Bottom left: A Wilson 0–6–0 from the OW & W. This was one of a batch built at the same time as the firm were supplying 2–2–2 and 2–4–0 passenger engines. This 0–6–0, which has had some of its boiler mountings " Great Westernised," was built in 1855, and had cylinders 16 in. by 22 in. and 4 ft. 6 in. coupled wheels.

Above: A typical E. B. Wilson 2–4–0 express locomotive from the OW & W, showing the classical fluted dome cover and safety valve column. Originally built in 1855, it had 6 ft. 6 in. coupled wheels and 16 in. by 22 in. cylinders. Like all Wilson's products these 2–4–0s were very soundly constructed and put in more than 30 years' service.

Below: An early product of the G. Armstrong regime. A 2–4–0 tank of 1865, showing the earlier bell-mouthed form of chimney and Joseph Armstrong's style of safety valve cover.

Above: A modification of one of Daniel Gooch's early standard-gauge designs, built at Swindon in 1862. .His earliest o 6–os for the standard gauge were built in 1855 and conveyed to Wolverhampton on special broad-gauge trucks. The engine illustrated was similar in having 5 ft. diameter coupled wheels but the cylinders were larger, 16 in. by 24 in. and they had Stephenson's link motion instead of Gooch's own valve gear.

Above left: A Wolverhampton rebuild of one of the latest and best West Midland express engines. The six engines of this class were built by Beyer, Peacock & Co. in 1862 and had 6 ft. coupled wheels, and 16 in. by 20 in. cylinders. In this rebuild, which dates from 1883, the unusual form of the cab side sheets will be noted.

Below: The south end of Stafford Road Works about 1880. It is interesting to try and " spot " some of the many types of locomotive outside. On the extreme right hand road is the Sharp 2–2–2 of 1848, behind what appears to be a tenderless Beyer of 1862 from the OW & W. Towards the left of the picture is a relatively " modern " domeless 2–2–2.

Top left: This 0–6–0 goods engine of the 322 class is notable as a representative of the last group of GWR locomotives to be built by an outside contractor until the French compound Atlantics came in 1903–5. The 332 class were entirely of Beyer, Peacock's own design, and were excellent and long-lived engines. There were 30 of them, built in 1864–6. The engine illustrated, No. 338, was afterwards rebuilt as a saddle-tank.

Middle left: The longevity of the 322 class is underlined by this illustration, which shows one of them as running in the Churchward era, with Belpaire firebox, and standard Dean-type boiler.

Bottom left: A long-lived survivor from the Birkenhead Railway: this little Fairbairn 2–4–0 of 1855 No. 106 is shown as rebuilt at Wolverhampton for the second time, about 1890. It was scrapped in 1900.

Top: Sister engine to No. 106, this ex-Birkenhead 2–4–0 is here shown after her first rebuilding at Wolverhampton in 1873. Both engines were used for many years in the Severn Valley line between Shrewsbury and Worcester. This engine in her final rebuilt form was not scrapped until 1905, having run 815,454 miles.

Above: A fascinating example of the miscellaneous collection of locomotives that came into GWR stock: a renewal of an 1850 Sharp, Stewart 0–6–0, built Newport in 1875, and belonging to the Monmouthshire Railway & Canal Company.

Above: A 3226 class 2–4–0 in 20th century style. Here No. 3228, with Belpaire firebox, is shown working a fast freight train through Patchway. This engine was scrapped in 1914.

Top left: The " Chancellor " class of 2–4–0, as originally built by George England & Co. of Hatcham in 1862. They had all the characteristics of Swindon broad-gauge days, with their sandwich frames, and Gooch-style boilers.

Middle left: Chancellor, as rebuilt at Wolverhampton. The class of eight locomotives was dealt with in 1878–1883, and were put to work on the North-West express service via the Severn Tunnel from its inception in 1888. As rebuilt they had 17 in. by 24 in. cylinders, 6 ft. 6 in. coupled wheels and a boiler pressure of 140 lb. per sq. in.

Bottom left: One of the Wolverhampton-built 2–4–0s of the 111 class, of 1866, in its original condition. They had 16 in. by 24 in. cylinders, and 6 ft. diameter coupled wheels, and were expressly designed for the stopping train services of the Northern Division.

Wolverhampton 2–4–0 varieties: some of these, like
Nos. 12, 444 and 722, were originally of Swindon
build, but later rebuilt to incorporate the unmis-
takable imprint of George Armstrong. No. 12 was a
handsome little thing of 1869 vintage, while No. 444
was of the so-called " Bicycle " class, dating from
1868. Originally the platforms along the side of the
engines was bent round the coupled wheels after the
style of broad-gauge coupled engines. This peculiar
appearance earned them their nickname. When
renewed at Wolverhampton in 1885 they were
completely modernised in appearance; but still
they were known as the " Bicycles ". No. 722 was a
6 ft. Swindon engine of 1872 shown as rebuilt.
Illustrations (bottom left) and (bottom right) show G.
Armstrong rebuilds of the celebrated West Midland
" Beyers " of 1861, originally 2–2–2s but when
rebuilt in 1883 changed to 2–4–0s. It will be seen
that No. 211 has acquired a raised-top firebox.
These engines continued to work on the former
OW & W line.

Left: An earlier, but equally typical Swindon 2–4–0 of the 481 class, of 1869. The photograph is of interest as showing many characteristic details of the mixed gauge era, such as the uniformity of the track ballasting, the substantial station buildings and the diminutive coaching stock.

Middle left: A characteristic Swindon-built 2–4–0 of 1873, No. 818, incorporating the generally favoured open splashers, but with the running plate lowered to a more conventional position than on the "Bicycle" class. The cab was added subsequently to the original construction.

Bottom left: This illustration shows one of the 111 class as later rebuilt to conform with the usual Wolverhampton style of the 1880s. The large legend

board on the Birmingham North signalbox will be noted as an incidental feature.

Above: Two 111s of the GWR: the prototype of the 111 class 2–4–0s of 1863 here rebuilt into the 20th century style, buffered up to Churchward's gigantic No. 111, the first British Pacific *The Great Bear.*

Below: A new 2–4–0 class of considerably greater power was introduced from Swindon in 1889, with 18 in. by 24 in. cylinders, but it was followed in the same year by a new Wolverhampton class, Nos. 3226–3231, with 17 in. by 24 in. cylinders and "slab" outside frames, instead of the usual "sandwich" type of Swindon. No. 3226 as originally built is shown here entering Snow Hill station, Birmingham, from the north.

Top: Saddle-tank 0–6–0 No. 126, rebuilt at Wolverhampton in 1881, from a Swindon 0–6–0 tender engine of 1862. It had 17½ in. by 24 in. cylinders, coupled wheels 4 ft. 7½ in. and was scrapped in 1928.

Above: Wolverhampton-built 0–6–0 saddle tank No. 1056 of 1871, first of a class of 10. It had 17½ in. by 24 in. cylinders, 4 ft. 7½ in. coupled wheels, and was converted to pannier tank in 1919.

Top: Wolverhampton-built 0–6–0 tank of 1894, originally a saddle-tank, with 16 in. by 24 in. cylinders and 4 ft. 1½ in. coupled wheels. It is here shown as converted to a pannier tank in 1910.

Above: Wolverhampton-built 0–6–0 side-tank engine of 1871, 633–644 class. It is here shown as rebuilt in 1902, with larger 17 in. by 24 in. cylinders, 4 ft. 7½ in. coupled wheels, and condensing gear, for working through the tunnels of the Inner Circle to Smithfield goods station, near Farringdon Street. Not scrapped until 1934.

One of the celebrated 69–76 class of 2–2–2 built at Wolverhampton 1872, but used mostly on turns operated from Swindon. They had 17 in. by 24 in. cylinders and 6 ft. 6 in. coupled wheels. Later illustrations in this book show engines of this class converted to 2–4–0s and named after rivers.

Swindon-built 2–2–2 express locomotive of the " Sir Daniel " class; 30 of these were built 1866–9, with 17 in. by 24 in. cylinders, and 7 ft. driving wheels. This illustration shows one of them as rebuilt at Wolverhampton. Three of the class were at one time working on the north main line and stationed at Birkenhead.

Below: One of the " Sir Daniel " class 2–2–2s in what might be termed " second state ", retaining the open splasher but fitted with Wolverhampton-type rolled top chimney, and cab.

Bottom: This photograph shows a " Sir Daniel " in the final state before the major rebuilding as 0–6–0 goods engines, with closed-in splasher, Swindon-type chimney top and large dome towards the forward end of the boiler.

Part Two

Southern Division — "Narrow" Gauge

Anyone familiar with the inner workings of the Great Western Railway in the 1870s and 1880s could not fail to have noticed a marked difference in the attitude towards the national standard gauge in the Northern and Southern Divisions of the line. At Wolverhampton the standard gauge *was* standard. Northern Division locomotives came alongside London & North Western and Midland trains at various points in their orbit, and although the crack London turns took them over a considerable mileage of mixed-gauge track, it was the broad gauge trains to be seen south and east of Didcot which were the odd men out. In the Southern Division things were very different. Although far-sighted men realised that the days of the broad gauge were numbered, officialdom preserved the most extraordinary attitude on the inherent and undying superiority of the broad gauge. There were many GWR men of the old school who believed, in all sincerity, that a narrow-gauge engine *could* not run so fast as a broad gauge, and the trains were timed accordingly.

It will be noted that I have begun to use the term " narrow gauge ", rather than " standard gauge ". To the broad-gauge faction there was no such thing as a British standard gauge; there were only two ways to regard gauges, and those were " broad " and " narrow ". It was perhaps as well that the timetable clerks of the 1870s and 1880s provided easy schedules for the narrow-gauge express trains, because the locomotives, excellent though they were in themselves, were not very powerful, even by the standards of the time. Whereas the broad-gauge " Flying Dutchman " and " Zulu " were booked to run the $77\frac{1}{4}$ miles from Paddington to Swindon in 87 minutes, non-stop, the very fastest narrow gauge train, the evening " New Milford Boat Train ", was allowed 97 minutes for the same run. On the up road one of the best narrow-gauge trains took 100 minutes from Swindon to Paddington, including a five-minute stop at Reading. This train, the 9.45 a.m. up ran the $41\frac{1}{4}$ miles to Reading in 50 minutes, start to stop, and took another 45 minutes over the final 36 miles to Paddington. Nevertheless these seemingly modest narrow-gauge timings taxed the capacity of the locomotives in two distinct ways. The traffic authorities used these narrow-gauge trains to convey much fast and priority goods traffic, as well as passengers. Milk vans, horseboxes and suchlike were added indiscriminately, and the loads were often quite heavy. The second handicap was less obvious.

Until the final changing of the gauge, in 1892, nearly all main lines in the Southern Division were laid with Brunel's longitudinal timber " baulk " road, with continuous support for the rails. That track was one of Brunel's less enlightened inventions. It was indescribably stiff and unyielding—as indeed he fully intended it should be; but it was a great handicap in locomotive running, and definitely limited traction capacity. Wolverhampton drivers of the 2-2-2 single engines illustrated in these pages, who ran regularly over sections of track laid on some stretches with the longitudinal baulks and elsewhere with transverse sleepered track, always insisted that their engines were " two coaches stronger " on the sleepered track. Yet in the Southern Division practically all the narrow-gauge express trains were run by 2–2–2 single engines, in rather pedestrian style.

While the traffic authorities in their time-table compilations, and the legacy from Brunel that remained in the track, effectively combined to preserve the myth of broad-gauge superiority, the locomotive department at Swindon had yet another way of holding the narrow-gauge engines on a tight rein. On other British railways of the period some locomotive engineers endeavoured to ensure that their engines were not worked uneconomically by using cylinders that were disproportionately large in relation to the boilers; so if a driver should attempt to thrash an engine, working at an uneconomical rate, he would quickly run himself short of steam. Swindon put the damper on such attempts— metaphorically, I hasten to add—in a rather more subtle way. The boilers were always excellent, and the cylinders somewhat on the small side; but the capacity of the engines was limited by use of an unusually large blastpipe. This made for a soft blast and easy running, with a complete absence of the fire-throwing from the chimney that was so prevalent on the LNWR and on the Great Northern. But while it made for economical running that large blast pipe orifice effectively put a check on any ardent spirit who had ideas about making up time; there was no means of sharpening the blast to increase the rate of evaporation in the boiler—unless of course a " jemmy " or " dart " was surreptitiously fixed in the blastpipe. While this was a common, albeit " under-the-counter " practice on some railways, with engines that would not steam freely it was virtually unheard of on the Great Western express engines of the 19th century.

The 2–2–2 engines that were doing almost all the express work on the standard gauge up to 1890 were of three classes, all with 7 ft. driving wheels:—

In their respective original conditions there would be no difficulty in distinguishing one from another. The " Sir Daniels " had domed boilers, slab outside frames, and open splashers, as shown in the picture of No. 586 on page 26–7. The " Sir Alexanders " had similar frames and splashers, but with the exception of the first engine of the class, which was named *Queen*, and frequently in demand for Royal trains, they had domeless boilers. The third class, while also having domeless boilers, was readily distinguishable from the others in having the old broad-gauge type of sandwich frames. To anyone riding on the footplate this type of frame had a natural springiness that seemed to compensate in some way for the stiffness of the " baulk road ", and gave these engines a certain advantage over the " Sir Alexanders ", although both had the same nominal tractive power.

Having said that the " Sir Daniels " and the " Sir Alexanders " were readily distinguishable I must add that in the course of their lives engines of both classes underwent several rebuildings, not in any ordered plan, but just as the exigencies of the day in Swindon Works happened to suit, when an individual engine came in for repairs. All eventually had their splashers closed in, but it was the multiplicity of boilers that so confused the issue. If one studies the pictures of *Sir Watkin* and *Prince Christian* on pages 28 and 36 it is indeed hard to discern that both are not of the same class. The only difference is in the shape of the sandbox just ahead of the driving wheel splasher. In the case of an approaching train, as in the picture on page 35, it is almost impossible to decide whether the engine is a " Sir Daniel " or a " Sir Alexander ". In 1899, however, William Dean put the " spotters " of that era out of their difficulties, by rebuilding all 30 engines of the " Sir Daniel " class as 0–6–0 goods engines! The frames, cylinders and motion were used, even to the extent of retaining the curved central portion of the running plate, which had previously arched over the driving wheel bearing.

The 157 class in their original condition, exemplified by the photograph of No. 158 on page 37, were much admired locomotives. I think it must have been the broad polished brass band of their open splashers that caught the eye, extended downwards on the trailing side to within a few inches of rail level. They also experienced the variations of boiler applied to the " Sir Alexanders " when the time came for rebuilding, or even routine heavy repair, and the pictures on pages 37 and 38 show two varieties: No. 162 *Cobham* has a neat, straightbacked, domed type, while the pioneer of the class No. 157, running a stopping train near Acton, after the final gauge conversion, has a boiler with a dome close behind the chimney and a raised top firebox. Some further variations of these popular engines are described in Part III of this book.

While general reliance was placed on the 71 singles of the 2–2–2 type, with 7 ft. driving wheels, there were two isolated engines having 7 ft. 8 in. wheels that could, in retrospect, have been considered as " feelers " towards what later became the standard express passenger engine of the whole railway. These 7 ft. 8 in. 2–2–2s were numbered 9 and 10, but differed greatly from each other. No. 9 shown on page 38, used odd bits, including the driving wheels, from a mysterious and unsuccessful 4–2–4 tank engine. In her more orthodox state No. 9 had a most peculiar arrangement of the Stephenson link motion. The eccentrics were outside, and drove the valves, located on top of the cylinders, through a rocking shaft mechanism, which frequently broke. In 1890 she was completely renewed as a 7 ft. 2–2–2 with outside slab frames, similarly to the " Sir Alexanders ". The other experimental 2–2–2 No. 10, built in 1886, could be described as a straightforward 7 ft. 8 in. version of the " Sir Alexanders ", with 18 in. by 26 in. cylinders. Although a faster and more reliable engine than No. 9, it was converted to a seven-footer in 1890.

Mention that the " Sir Daniel " class were converted into 0–6–0 goods engines leads on to the development of the standard GWR goods design, from the outside-framed Armstrong engines of 1866. There were no fewer than 300 of this class built over a period of about ten years, and they had boilers, cylinders, and motion interchangeable with the 2–2–2 " single " express engines. This excellent design was the forerunner of the celebrated " Dean Goods ", the first of which was built at Swindon in 1883. At that time there was a definite vogue for domeless boilers at Swindon, as shown in the " Sir Alexander "and " 157 " classes of 2–2–2. The first 20 of the " Dean Goods ", Nos. 2301–2320 had domeless boilers, but inside frames. The cylinders were still 17 ins. by 24 in., as on the Armstrong engines. There did seem some uncertainty as to whether to standardise on inside frames, and the third and fourth batches of these engines, built in 1885 and 1886, had outside frames. But it was only the first 20 that had domeless boilers. Construction of what became the standard type, with inside frames, and domed boilers, continued unbrokenly from 1890 to 1899, at the end of which latter year the running numbers had reached 2580, representing a stud of 280 excellent engines. It would perhaps be invidious to suggest that they were the best 0–6–0 goods engines ever built; but in their final form with superheater boilers and Belpaire fireboxes, as shown in the illustration of No. 2370, they were certainly one of the liveliest medium-power *mixed traffic* engines ever to run the rails, as British Railways found to their consternation soon after nationalisation when comparison came to be made on the Swindon testing plant with a new type of 2–6–0 tender engine ostensibly equipped with all the latest " mod cons ".

A curious future was meted out to 20 of these engines, in 1907–1910. Apparently there was needed a still lighter 2–6–2 tank engine than the new standard 45XX having outside cylinders and taper boiler, and so Churchward took the Dean Goods, fitted pony trucks fore and aft, and put on a non-superheated taper boiler. An outstanding and ugly feature was the use of very long side tanks, which had a capacity 50 per cent greater than those of the 45XX outside cylinder 2–6–2s. This may have been the purpose of the conversion; but it did not produce a very handsome engine. As Part III of this book shows, however, the fitting of modern domeless boilers to older engines, no matter how more efficient they were in service, did not improve the appearance of the very graceful 19th century engines of the GWR; and the metamorphosis of these 20 engines of the Dean goods series was merely a case in point, even if a somewhat exceptional one.

The little " Metro " tanks of the GWR were very familiar engines to commuters in the London area right down to the 1930s, when I personally travelled behind them daily between Ealing Broadway and Bishops Road. Joseph Armstrong's original version, of 1869, will be less familiar, with inside frames throughout as shown in the illustration of No. 457, and the running plate valence shaped to give access to the crank pins, even in the uppermost position. But while No. 457 shows the unfamiliar aspect of a class that afterwards became very familiar, the 4–4–0 No. 3552, also illustrated, was one of a class that had a truly extraordinary early life. There were surely few British 4–4–0s that began as 0–4–2 saddle tanks, and having withstood two early conversions, including the rail gauge, were then turned round, end for end, and changed from a 0–4–4 into a 4–4–0! The result was certainly a class of smart little engines, but one could wonder if the work concerned in such a conversion was justified by the utilisation subsequently obtained. Actually these 4–4–0s had long lives, and some even received standard taper boilers with superheaters. The Swindon version of the ubiquitous 0–6–0 saddle tank was also a long-lived and good revenue-earning unit.

In the 19th century, when so much interest was being displayed in compound locomotives, Great Western adventures into this field were few, and unsuccessful. From the accompanying illustration of 2–4–0 No. 7 it would hardly be imagined that it was a four-cylinder compound. But the cylinders were all inside, arranged tandem-wise, with one high and one low pressure driving on to a common piston rod. Although this arrange-

ment preserved the traditional neatness of exterior that characterised the Dean era at Swindon, the details produced a sluggish and unreliable locomotive that spent most of its active days on slow trains between Swindon and Cardiff. After eight years of struggling— 1886–1894—the engine was rebuilt as a 4–4–0 (see page 45).

Rebuilds amounting to metamorphoses seemed popular at Swindon at the end of last century. I have already mentioned the conversion of the " Sir Daniel " class 2–2–2s into 0–6–0 goods engines, quite apart from the case of the 4–4–0s Nos. 3521–60, and the tandem compound No. 7. Then there was the very fine Armstrong 69 class of 2–2–2s. In 1895–6 these were converted into 2–4–0 express engines, and as by that time naming was becoming a regular instead of an isolated practice on standard-gauge locomotives, this class received names, of rivers in country served by the GWR. There must have been a restricting limit to the length of the names chosen. Anything longer than five letters would have disappeared behind the outside spring hangars. At that time it was customary to mount the nameplates on, rather than above the splashers. Fortunately for the nomenclature department at Swindon the West of England and the West Midlands had a plentiful supply of short river names, and it was able to leave out the two longest rivers, Thames and Severn. The actual names used were *Avon, Dart, Dee, Exe, Isis, Stour, Teign* and *Wye*. This still left the Fal and Tamar as spares!

In the Dean era the running department seemed to find considerable use for 2–4–0 and 4–4–0 engines with very small driving wheels and even, as previously mentioned, had a whole class of tank engines rebuilt for the purpose. In 1885 a class of five little 2–4–0s was built new in this category, Nos. 3201–5. They were powerful little engines, with 17 in. by 26 in. cylinders, carrying a boiler pressure of 150 lb. per sq. in., and acquired the nickname of the " Stella " class—how, I have never discovered. But in an age of standardisation three of these engines survived into the

1930s, in a form that will be mentioned later. The photograph of No. 3204 is of particular interest as it was taken at Manchester Exchange (LNWR). Until World War I there were regular GWR locomotive workings between Chester and Manchester, having regard to the line between Chester and Warrington being jointly owned by the two companies. At one time one of the principal LNWR expresses from Manchester to the North Wales coast was worked by a Great Western engine as far as Chester.

Variety in Swindon designs of passenger 2–4–0s is well illustrated by the photographs of Nos. 2213, 3216, and 3251 on pages 44 and 45. The 2210–2220 series of 1882, illustrated in original condition, had the usual 17 in. by 24 in. cylinders of the day, and displayed that seeming uncertainty on Swindon's part as to whether to have domed, or domeless boilers. In 1889, however, having built engines with straight, inside frames, though matched with tenders of the sandwich frame type, they reverted to slotted outside frames for the celebrated "Barnum" class, Nos. 3206–3225. These had 18 in. by 24 in. cylinders and 6 ft. 2 in. coupled wheels. These were extremely useful and long-lived engines, as were also the 3232 class of 1892–3. These latter were real express engines, having 6 ft. 8 in. coupled wheels; they were used on the West to North trains, via the Severn Tunnel, and in later years some of them were fitted with superheated domed boilers. Although one of them was scrapped in 1918 general withdrawal of the class did not begin until 1923, and then it was no more than gradual. Seven out of the original 20 were still in service in 1928.

The final conversion of the broad gauge in 1892 released Swindon from the incubus of an interim or convertible policy. The burden must have been severe—to keep the railway running up to the last minute with a considerable broad-gauge mileage, and yet to have on hand sufficient locomotives to take over on the standard gauge overnight, as it were. But having eliminated the broad gauge from May 1892, the GWR entered into the final flowering of the Dean era, in a series of locomotives of elegant appearance and excellent performance. The "Duke of Cornwall" class of 1895 may not have been the most handsome, being distinguished by a long extended smokebox and very short tenders. They were designed especially to work west of Newton Abbot, beyond which the "single" express engines did not penetrate. In broad-gauge days the South Devon and Cornwall lines had been worked exclusively by saddle-tank 4–4–0 engines, and some of the turntables down in the West were accordingly short. But as motive power units the 'Dukes' were quite first class, with 18 in. by 26 in. cylinders, 5 ft. $7\frac{1}{2}$ in. coupled wheels and a boiler pressure of 160 lb. per sq. in. In later years the nameplates were changed to the familiar curved type, over the top of the splashers; but in their early days the problem of display, which would have been even more difficult than on the 2–4–0 "Rivers", was solved by placing the names horizontally on the centre line of the boiler barrel.

The very pronounced extended smokeboxes of the "Duke" class were not used on the earlier Dean passenger engines of the "all-narrow-gauge" period. The four 4–4–0 express engines of the "Armstrong" class, dating from 1894, were extremely handsome though the boilers were not really large enough to supply cylinders 20 in. diameter by 26 in. stroke. They were later lined up to 19 in. and even then were a little on the large size for a hard-working engine. The four engines of this class were all replacements of older, and comparatively unsuccessful engines and the new No. 7 *Armstrong* may be compared with the tandem compound 2–4–0 of the same number, page 43. The other three engines of the class were named *Gooch*, *Charles Saunders* and *Brunel*, and between them honoured the greatest men in the past history of the GWR.

By the year 1896 the winds of change were beginning to blow through Swindon Works, and in that year the quite revolutionary 4–6–0 goods engine No. 36 was produced. Superficially this large engine could be described as a 4–6–0 development of the "Dean goods " and " Duke " style; but there was a good deal more to it than that. Dimensionally it was a heavy load hauler, with 4 ft. 7½ in. coupled wheels, 20 in. by 24 in. cylinders, and a boiler pressure of 165 lb. per sq. in.; but it was in respect of the boiler that the more subtle development was to be seen, in the downward extension of the raised top firebox to a wide grate, having an area of no less than 35 sq. ft. This would have been nothing unusual on American locomotives of that date; but in Great Britain it was outstanding. Then, as ever since, the gradients of the Severn Tunnel were a continual bugbear in freight train operation, but with No. 36 it was found possible to work a train of 30 loaded wagons and two brake vans through the tunnel in 11 minutes. The previous standard load of 35 wagons and two vans had always required two 0–6–0 engines, and the time was 18 to 20 minutes. So in tractive power No. 36 represented a big advance.

To railway enthusiasts, and particularly those living on or near the West of England main line, the principal attractions were the beautiful Dean 7 ft. 8 in. " single " express engines, all of which eventually had names. The earliest of them had begun life as the ugliest imaginable " convertibles ", taking turns, just before the final conversion of the gauge, with the Gooch 8 ft. 4–2–2s. But then, like the ugly duckling of the legend, they were transformed into the most elegant of swans, passing through a somewhat shaky initial period as narrow-gauge 2–2–2s on the way. The first eight engines of the class were built as " convertibles " in 1891 and numbered 3021–8. These were followed by two more, also in 1891, but for the standard gauge, and these two engines Nos. 3029–30 appeared in the form shown in the illustration of No. 3023. In 1892 a further batch of 20 standard gauge 2–2–2s was completed at Swindon, and numbered 3001–3020. The engine wheelbase was rather long, and to compensate for this the leading axleboxes were given a side play of 2 in. It was while running in this condition that one of them became derailed in a somewhat alarming manner inside the Box Tunnel in

September 1893; as a consequence it was decided to replace the leading axle by a four-wheeled bogie, and the engines then assumed their later and most graceful form.

In the meantime naming was in progress, mounting the names on the face of the splashers in the style of the " River " class rebuilt 2–4–0. Many of the names were perpetuations of those previously borne by the broad gauge 4–2–2s. Of the 80 engines of the 3001 class no fewer than 20 names had formerly graced the Gooch eight-footers. This to some extent was following the LNWR tradition of engine naming; but on the GWR it had no sooner been inaugurated than it was ended. So far as the Dean 7 ft. 8 in. singles were concerned, it is noticeable that all the names associated with the Crimean War were not used again, while 12 engines were named after members of the Royal family. Some of the most satisfying of the new names were those associated with the West Country and its people, such as *White Horse*, *Westward Ho*, *Devonia*, *Lorna Doone*, and again *Sir Francis Drake* and *Sir Richard Greenville*. Like all assorted groups of names, such as those of the LNWR, some laid themselves open to misconception. For example, engine No. 3055, originally *Trafalgar*, was renamed *Lambert*. Those knowing something of Great Western history might well connect this name with the heroic diver, whose courage at a highly critical moment enabled work to be restarted in constructing the Severn Tunnel after a disastrous burst-in of flood water. Actually, however, No. 3055 was named after one of the General Managers of the company, and could be coupled in this respect with names given to No. 3042 *Frederick Saunders* and No. 3056 *Wilkinson*. One of the pictures shows *Lambert* in all its glory, while another shows No. 3078 carrying its original name of *Shooting Star*. This had to be renamed when the new Churchward " Stars " were built in 1907, and it is interesting to find that No. 3078 then received one of the old broad-gauge 8-footer names that had so far not been used again, *Eupatoria*.

In the Churchward era many of these

34

engines underwent detail modifications, quite apart from those receiving domeless boilers, as related in the next section of this book. The illustration of No. 3043 *Hercules* shows what was perhaps the most modern form that those with domed boilers assumed. *Hercules* has the high raised Belpaire firebox, top feed, and both dome and safety valve cover painted over green. To provide an adequate look-out beside the firebox casing the wider cab of the "Atbara" and "City" class 4–4–0s has been fitted, encasing also the springs for the trailing wheels. She has also the more modern tender. Detail changes apart, the Dean "singles" were extremely fast engines, and participated fully in the exciting "Race from the West" in 1904, which took the "narrow-gauge" Great Western completely out of its 19th century leisure to the foremost place among British speed record-breakers.

A celebrated narrow-gauge express passing Acton. This is the pioneer corridor train, 1.30 p.m. Paddington to Birkenhead, introduced in 1892. Mixed gauge track still in use, though the outermost rail, providing for the broad gauge, does not seem so well used as the others. The engine is a "Sir Alexander" class 2–2–2.

Top: The difficulty of readily distinguishing the "Sir Daniel" from the "Sir Alexander" class will be well apparent from this photograph of No. 1118 *Prince Christian*, after the latter had been fitted with domed boiler. The only immediate clue is the shape of the sandbox, and below this is a step for access to the running plate. This was not fitted on the "Sir Daniel" class.

Below: Engine No. 473 of the "Sir Daniel" class as converted into a 0–6–0 goods engine, in 1900. The original curved form of the running plate is clearly seen, while the extensive rivetting on the original frame gives some indication of the way they had to be patched.

Top: One of the handsome 157 class in original condition, as built in 1879. The very broad brass band over the driving wheel splasher was a notable feature in itself, but this picture shows clearly how this splasher was extended below the running plate.

Below: A celebrated member of the 157 class, as rebuilt with domed boiler and closed-in splashers. This engine was a favourite on the London–Birmingham expresses of the 1890s, so much so that the class as a whole was sometimes referred to as the "Cobhams". No. 162 was, however, one of the first of the class to be scrapped, in 1904.

Left: Pioneer engine of the " Cobham " class, No. 157, on a stopping train near Acton in early narrow-gauge days. The engine has a raised-top firebox and represented one of several varieties of boilers fitted. This engine was scrapped in 1903.

Below left: The unique 7 ft. 8 in. 2–2–2 engine No. 9, rebuilt at Swindon in this form in 1884, from the experimental 4–2–4 tank engine. This photograph shows clearly the *outside* eccentrics and rods for actuating the *inside* valves.

Below: Engine No. 9 as rebuilt a second time in 1890 with 7 ft. driving wheels, conventional valve gear and outside slab frames. At this time the engine was named *Victoria*. It is shown here approaching Acton, at a time when all traces of the broad gauge and the " baulk road " had been removed. This engine was scrapped in 1905.

Above: One of the outside framed Dean goods 0–6–0s in its most modern form with Belpaire firebox and superheated boiler. The superheater had six elements, with a heating surface of 75.3 sq. ft.

Middle right: The GWR 0–6–0 goods engine: one of Joseph Armstrong's 388 class, which for many years was the narrow-gauge standard.

Top right: The very earliest form of the famous " Dean Goods " 0–6–0 was built in 1883 with domeless boiler. The neatly stacked pile of coal on the tender shows the traditional " large lump " quality of Welsh coal used on the GWR.

Bottom: An Armstrong standard 0–6–0 goods of the 388 class rebuilt with Dean boiler, passing Bathampton with a down train. This photograph shows well the condition of spotless cleanliness in which even goods engines were kept.

Far left: The original form of the famous 2–4–0 " Metro " tanks, as introduced by Joseph Armstrong in 1869. The driver seems well protected against cold weather—not by the " cab " but by his clothing!

Left: William Dean's experimental tandem compound 2–4–0 in 1886. The two high-pressure cylinders were 15 in. by 21 in. and the two low pressure 23 in. by 21 in., coupled wheels were 7 ft. diameter, boiler pressure 180 lb. per sq. in. Converted to 4–4–0 simple engine in 1894.

Below left: One of the remarkable 3521 class rebuilds: this engine originated as a broad-gauge saddle tank 0–4–2 in 1888; it was then altered to the 0–4–4 type, still broad-gauge, in 1890. In 1892 it was converted to standard gauge, and in 1900 completely turned about to become a 4–4–0 tender engine.

Below: An interesting shot of one of the 1885–6 batch of Dean goods 0–6–0s, having outside frames. This photograph shows a southbound goods passing over Lapworth water troughs, between Lapworth and Hatton.

Top: A " Dean Goods " rebuilt as a 2–6–2 tank. Twenty of these engines, Nos. 2491–2510, originally built in 1896 were rebuilt in the form shown in 1907–1910. They were renumbered 3901–3920, though not in the exact order of the original numbers. Although having the Churchward short-cone taper boiler, they were not originally superheated.

Above: The Swindon version of the outside-framed saddle tank 0–6–0 built 1886. In one respect the 1661 class, of which there were 40, were distinct in having 17 in. by 26 in. cylinders, in contrast to nearly all GWR 0–6–0 tank engines of the 19th century, which had 17 in. by 24 in. cylinders.

Top right: One of the handsome 69 class 2–2–2s as rebuilt 2–4–0 of the " River " class. This engine was converted at Swindon in 1896.

Middle right: Even on this small class of rebuilds there seems to have been no uniformity of boilers. No. 72 *Dee* has a different boiler from No. 69, the former having the dome in a forward position, and a slightly extended smokebox.

Bottom right: A " Stella " class 2–4–0 with new boiler and Belpaire firebox, giving it a strong family likeness to the neo-Dean style of the 20th century, on domed-boiler engines.

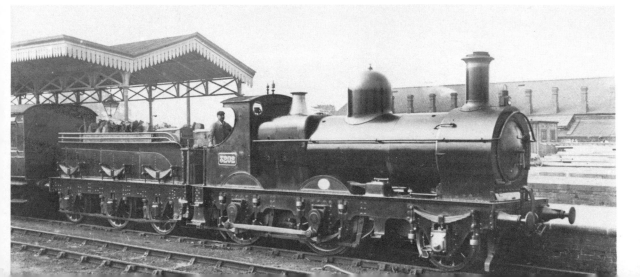

Top left: Modernised version of the 3232 class, as running until the mid-1920s. Engine No. 3245 has a superheated Belpaire boiler, with the usual six-element superheater fitted to boilers of this type. No. 3245 was scrapped in September 1926.

Middle left: A 2–4–0 express engine of the 3232 class of 1892–3 having 17½ in. by 24 in. cylinders, 6 ft. 8½ in. coupled wheels, and used on the West to North expresses via the Severn Tunnel.

Bottom left: Further 2–4–0 varieties: a 2210 class express passenger engine, No. 2213, in original condition as built in 1882, with inside frames for the driving wheels, " straightback " domeless boiler, but tender with outside slotted frames.

Below: One of the celebrated " Barnum " mixed traffic 2–4–0s of 1889, in original condition. An incidental peculiarity of these engines was that they had tenders with cut-away plate frames as later standardised, although the engines themselves had the old-style slotted frames. For the sake of uniformity one might suggest that classes 2210 and 3206 might have exchanged tenders!

Bottom: The one-time tandem compound 2–4–0 rebuilt. This handsome engine, named *Armstrong*, had 20 in. by 26 in. cylinders, originally, and the type of boiler that became standard on the 7 ft. 8 in. singles.

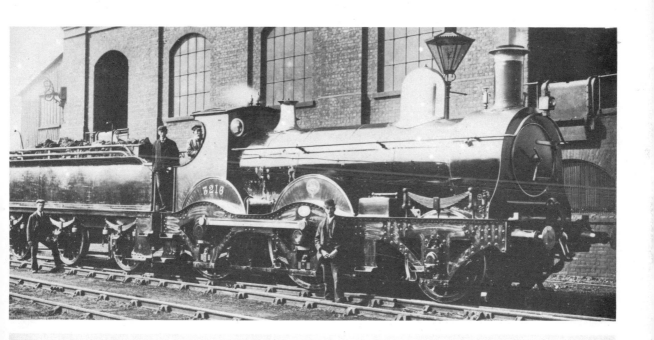

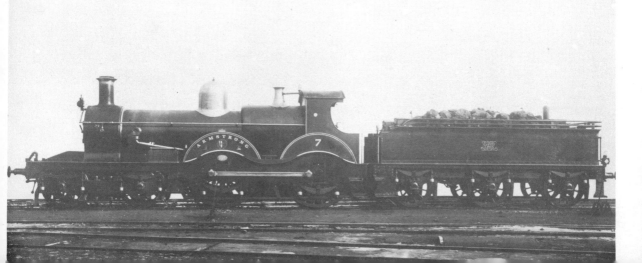

Top: One of the 481 class of 2–4–0s, originally built at Swindon in 1869, and extensively used on the " Berks and Hants " line between Reading and Trowbridge, here shown rebuilt with boiler having Belpaire firebox, but retaining the old style of number plate. This photograph makes an interesting comparison with the original form of these engines, as shown on page 22.

Above: A second engine of the 7 ft. 4–4–0 quartet, No. 14 *Charles Saunders*. This was a rebuild of a broad-gauge convertible 2–4–0 of 1888. But in the " conversion ", after May 1892, the engine was rebuilt to conform with the *Armstrong* ex-compound rehabilitation.

Top: A striking broadside view of the original form of the " Duke " class 4–4–0, showing the abnormally long extended smokebox, horizontal form of nameplate and very short tender. Engine No. 3260 *Merlin* was one of the first batch, 3252–3261, built at Swindon in 1895.

Middle: The earliest narrow-gauge form of the Dean 7 ft. 8 in. singles, as a 2–2–2, unnamed, and

rebuilt from the convertible design of 1891. This engine, No. 3023, was afterwards named *Swallow*.

Bottom: The Dean 7 ft. 8 in. single at the height of its elegance. Engine No. 3055, built March 1895, and then named *Trafalgar*. Renamed *Lambert* in 1901. It was fitted with a domed boiler with Belpaire firebox in 1913, but scrapped in the following year.

Top: **Engine No. 3078** *Shooting Star,* built February 1899, and renamed *Eupatoria* in 1906. This engine retained the original type of boiler throughout until scrapped in November 1911.

Above: The most modern form of the domed 7 ft. 8 in. singles: No. 3043 *Hercules,* built January 1895, fitted with boiler having Belpaire firebox in 1913, but scrapped later in the same year.

Bottom: The first GWR 4–6–0: Dean's experimental heavy mineral engine No. 36, of 1896, with 4 ft. 7½ in. coupled wheels, 20 in. by 24 in. cylinders, and a boiler pressure of 165 lb. per sq. in. Note the firebox, wide at the bottom, and providing a grate area of 35 sq. ft.

Above right: One of the " Stella " class of 2–4–0, Nos. 3201-5 built in 1885, here shown at Manchester Exchange station, LNWR. Apart from the family party in front of the tender, note should be taken of the massive stacking up of coal on the small tender, using huge slabs to extend the side supports and enable the smaller coal to be piled high inside.

Right: Another engine of the one-time convertible batch No. 3022, named *Rougemont.* Despite their tractive capacity, these engines were often double-headed on the heaviest express trains, as in this picture. This engine was converted to the 4–2–2 type in 1894, and renamed *Bessemer* in 1898.

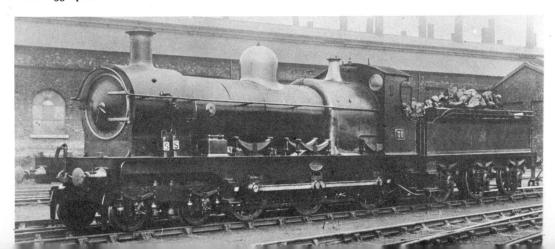

Below: The " Badminton " class 4–4–0 with domeless parallel boiler and high raised Belpaire firebox No. 3310 *Waterford*, built 1899. This engine had an unusual feature in the tail-lever attached to the safety valves.

Bottom: The ponderous domeless boilered 4–6–0 No. 2601. Note the groups of helical springs above the running plate, the combustion chamber ahead of the firebox proper and the large " saddle-tank " sandbox on the boiler. Built Swindon 1899.

Part Three

The Churchward Evolution

In presenting a notable paper to the Institution of Mechanical Engineers in February 1906, G. J. Churchward began with these words: " The modern locomotive problems is principally a question of boiler. The great increase in the size of boilers, and of the pressures carried, which has taken place during the past few years has necessitated reconsideration of the principles of design which had been worked out and settled during many years' experience with comparatively small boilers carrying low pressures. The higher temperatures incidental to the higher pressures have required the provision of much more liberal water spaces and better provision for circulation . . ." In referring to " the great increase in the size of boilers ", his paper quickly showed it was the USA and not Great Britain he had in mind—certainly not his own GWR. He then went on to emphasise the constraint put upon British locomotive designers by the relative smallness of the loading gauge, but it is now well known that for some years before he succeeded William Dean as Locomotive, Carriage and Wagon Superintendent his influence in design was becoming progressively stronger and in no field more so than with boilers.

The first subtle difference from traditional Swindon boiler design was to be seen as early as 1897 in the " Badminton " class 4–4–0s, which although having a domed boiler in the style of the 7 ft. 8 in. singles had a Belpaire firebox, with its top considerably above the line of the boiler barrel. The design was strongly criticised for its angular appearance,

and it was perpetuated in the new 5 ft. 8 in. 4–4–0 *Bulldog*, which was completed at Swindon in 1898. In these new engines the aim was to give increased steam space in the hottest part of the boiler, that is, just above the crown sheet of the firebox proper. This in turn promoted greater circulation within the boiler, and consequently freer steaming. At the same time Churchward was already thinking of dispensing with the dome. The aperture giving access to it was inherently a source of weakness in the boiler structure, quite apart from that arising from such inordinately large domes as had come into fashion at Swindon in the 1890s. With Churchward thinking in terms of higher pressures—though not as yet exerting his increasing influence to get them actually adopted on the GWR—it was naturally desirable to keep the mechanical structure of the boiler as simple as possible.

There was plenty of experience with domeless boilers in the GWR, but all so far in the era of leisurely running, when locomotives were not steamed at their maximum for any appreciable time. Then the last-but-one of the " Badminton " class 4–4–0s, engine No. 3310 *Waterford*, was fitted with a large domeless boiler and Belpaire firebox. There was something about that firebox that gave a clue towards future development: its sides were not entirely vertical, but sloped slightly outwards from the top. *Waterford* was in many ways a more graceful engine than the standard " Badmintons ", but in 1899 lovers of the aesthetic in locomotive lineaments got a savage jolt from the appearance from Swindon of the second GWR 4–6–0, No. 2601. This could be described as a domeless boilered development of the pioneer 4–6–0 No. 36 (page 50) but an uglier engine can scarcely ever have run the rails. It had all the angularity of a parallel domeless boiler, and high raised Belpaire firebox, with the added accompaniment of a combustion chamber ahead of the firebox proper, and above all a huge sandbox on the top of the boiler, just abaft the smokebox, and shaped like a saddle tank, with a flat top. The *Locomotive Magazine* described this engine in its issue of February 1900, with bated breath it seemed, but without any illustration. It seemed as though the editor was fearful of revealing to what depths of iconoclasm Swindon had descended, and readers other than those living near the GWR had to wait until the following December for a first glimpse of No. 2601. This was functionalism with a vengeance, and it was followed in 1901 by the 2–6–0 development, no less ugly, and sarcastically nicknamed " Kruger ", in reference to our late enemy in the Transvaal!

Happily these extremes of angularity were not extended to the passenger engines, when domeless boilers and high raised Belpaire fireboxes were applied to new standard types of 4–4–0 with both 5 ft. 8 in. and 6 ft. 8 in. driving wheels. The first of the former was No. 3352, named *Camel*, and it embodied a new, but transient style of number and nameplates. The name was carried on an oval plate at the cab side, which included the number in relatively small figures, and the company's coat of arms in the centre. As the number was rather small it was repeated in a larger plate on the centre line of the smokebox. In these engines also the traditional copper-capped chimney disappeared, and was replaced by a shapely, outward-tapering, cast-iron design. It could not be said that *Camel* was an ugly engine; it was just that it was *different*.

The year 1900 was a notable one for the GWR. It witnessed the introduction of three new locomotive types, all with domeless parallel boilers and high raised Belpaire fireboxes. The first was a more shapely development of the " Krugers ". These latter had the unusual cylinder dimensions of 19 in. diameter by 28 in. stroke, but in the development of 1900 this was changed to 18 in. by 26 in. Aesthetically the most welcome change was the removal of that hideous sandbox, while the firebox did not have the forward-thrusting combustion chamber. The first of these new engines, which was followed by a further 33 in 1901, was painted in the full passenger colours of the day, with light red underframes, and all the usual brass work. Like the " Camels," however, they had plain cast iron chimneys. They were designed for the heavy coal traffic from South Wales, and were always known as the " Aberdares ". The second new type of 1900 was a 2–4–2 tank engine for the increasingly heavy outer suburban traffic. As in the case of the " Aberdares " only one prototype was built at first, and multiplication of this successful design did not begin until 1902.

There was no question of a single prototype with the third new design of 1900, the celebrated " Atbara " class of 4–4–0 express engine. Although new in appearance these splendid engines were really a synthesis of recently introduced Swindon features, including the straight-barrelled domeless boiler, Belpaire firebox, and " engine " layout as in the " Badmintons ". The cylinders were the same, 18 in. by 26 in., and so was the boiler pressure, 180 lb. per sq. in. But there were some improvements in valve design, in addition to the increased steaming capacity of the boiler, which made the " Atbaras " extremely free running engines. C. Rous-Marten recorded maximum speeds of more than 90 m.p.h. with them. A pronounced external feature that is prominent in the broadside view of the pioneer engine on page 62, is the straight line of the running plate above the outside cranks.

By the time Churchward succeeded Dean as Locomotive, Carriage and Wagon Superintendent, the new form of boiler and firebox was becoming well proved, not only in its increased steaming capacity but in reduced maintenance costs, and in the following years boilers of this type were fitted to a number of older engines that still had a reasonable expectancy of useful life. There are, between pages 60 — 65, examples of no fewer than six classes fitted with these boilers, namely the "Barnum" 2–4–0—a very familiar type around Reading in my boyhood—the "Stella" 2–4–0, and the further rebuild of the latter as a 4–4–0, and then that of the Armstrong class 4–4–0 No. 16 *Brunel*. The result in this latter case was not very happy artistically, and still less so was the application of domeless boilers to some of the single-wheelers. Another picture shows the effect on one of the 2–2–2s of the 157 class, while yet another shows a 7 ft. 8 in. 4–2–2 thoroughly modernised.

There were originally 40 of the "Atbara" class 4–4–0s, built at Swindon in 1900–1901; but in 1902 Churchward took one of them, No. 3405 *Mauritius*, and fitted it with an entirely new type of domeless boiler. Instead of being parallel the barrel was coned. The idea was not by any means new—in fact it had been fairly common practice in the USA for many years; but rarely can it have been applied in so scientific a manner. The barrel was coned outwards so as to meet almost the full height and width of the Belpaire firebox, and so to give extra space, at a critical location, for circulation of the water, and for collection of steam above the water line. Furthermore, the firebox itself was more elaborately shaped than the plain box-like form of the ordinary Belpaire. All corners were carefully rounded, and care was taken to avoid having abrupt changes of shape that could give rise to local heating, and leaking joints and tubes. The rebuilt *Mauritius* was indeed prototype of the ever-famous "City" class of 1903, the pioneer engine of which No. 3433 *City of Bath* had not long been in service before she made a record non-stop run from Paddington to Plymouth, with a Royal special. The picture of *City of Truro* shows what these engines looked like in their original condition, while the later picture of the *City of Bath* taken after copper-capped

chimneys were coming into fashion again, shows clearly the rounded shape of the Belpaire firebox.

The "Camel" series of 5 ft. 8 in. 4–4–0s became incorporated in the "Bulldog" class, a later member of which is shown in the illustration of No. 3466 *Barbados*. This has the straight frames, taper boiler, and shaped Belpaire firebox used on the "Cities", while retaining the plain cast iron chimney still standard when this particular engine was built, in 1904. By that time also the modern form of nameplate mounting had been evolved, and although the general appearance is not so elaborate as in the Dean era, there are still a number of ornamental touches such as the polished brass edging on the bogie wheel splashers, and the polished brass caps on the spring hangers.

Ten of the "Atbaras" were rebuilt as "City" class, with the same design of taper boiler as fitted initially to *Mauritius*. These mostly bore names of cities in the British Empire overseas, and although they were fitted with nameplates of the type shown on *Barbados*, they were not prefixed with the words "City of". These engines, for the record, were *Durban*, *Halifax*, *Hobart*, *Lyttleton*, *Melbourne* and *Quebec*. There were some further "cities" among the "Atbaras", such as Auckland, Sydney, and Cape Town; but the remaining engines transferred to the "City" class proper were *Gibralter*, *Malta* and *Killarney*, in addition to the prototype, *Mauritius*. Another photograph shows one of the "Atbaras" in its finally developed form, with taper boiler, superheater and top feed. The original style of nameplate was retained to the end of the lives of these engines. The boilers fitted to them were smaller than those of the "Cities", and the "Atbaras" were later grouped with the new "Flower" class and the reboilered 'Badmintons' and 'Armstrongs' to form the comprehensive "Flower" class, all having the smaller version of the taper boiler.

Brilliant though the early performances of the "Atbara" and "City" class 4–4–0s were, these were never intended to become a

55

standard passenger express type. The policy of the Great Western management was to develop, for all it was worth, the great potential holiday traffic to the West of England, winter and summer alike, and at the same time to enhance the prestige of its train services by making many long non-stop runs. As Locomotive, Carriage and Wagon Superintendent, Churchward had a two-fold task: to provide locomotives capable of pulling far heavier loads than previously standard, at considerably higher average speeds, and at the same time to improve the economy of their working so that the coal consumption would not be such as to exhaust the fireman on a non-stop run of three hours or more. A collateral part of his overall responsibilities was to design new main-line coaching stock that would have lower rolling resistance per ton of dead weight, and thus further ease the burden of the locomotive and the fireman. That Churchward was a close student of American practice was evident from his well-documented references to it in the paper "Large Locomotive Boilers" previously mentioned, and in building the first Great Western passenger 4–6–0 American influence was apparent in the sudden switch to outside cylinders.

William Dean was still in office when the 4–6–0 No. 100 appeared, in 1902; but there was ample evidence of Churchward's influence. That inside Stephenson link motion was used was fully in keeping with current American practice, while the boiler and firebox could be described as "enlarged Atbara". The taper-boiler development seen on the "City" class 4–4–0s was applied to the second GWR express passenger 4–6–0, No. 98, built in 1903. But while this had the specially shaped Belpaire firebox used on the "Cities", the coning of the boiler barrel applied only to the rear portion, and in relation to later practice this design became known as the "short cone" boiler. Churchward was, however, leading the Swindon boiler shop gently and gradually towards the ultimate ideal of the fully coned boiler. On No. 98 also the pressure was raised to 200 lb.

per sq. in. for the first time on a Swindon-built locomotive. Nevertheless, while attending to the paramount need to give his drivers plenty of steam, there was equally a requirement to economise in its usage, and thoughts turned towards compounding, which was giving such remarkable results on the Northern Railway of France.

Churchward himself was by no means sold on compounding, and in building engine No. 98 he set out to produce a simple that was equal in thermal efficiency to a compound. This he virtually succeeded in doing, by making the cylinder stroke long in relation to the bore—18 in. by 30 in.—and by fitting large-diameter piston valves that had long laps and an unusually long travel in full gear. Even so, he was not sufficiently satisfied to dismiss compounding without an actual trial, and a De Glehn Four-cylinder compound Atlantic was purchased. This fine engine, the *La France*, was virtually a replica of the Atlantics then doing such splendid work on the Nord. It carried a boiler pressure of 227 lb. per sq. in., and Churchward built another 4–6–0 of his own, similar to No. 98, but having a boiler pressure of 225 lb. per sq. in. This was No. 171, and having regard to its competitive position in regard to the Frenchman it was named *Albion*. To put the trials on the fairest possible basis this engine was subsequently altered temporarily to the Atlantic type, in 1904.

Thirteen more Atlantics identical to the converted *Albion* were built in 1905, while six further engines were built in the same year as 4–6–0s. There was thus a trial period when engines of similar capacity were running, some as 4–4–2s and some as 4–6–0s. At the end of 1905 in fact the GWR had more Atlantics than 4–6–0s, for in addition to the 14 Swindon-built engines, there were three French compounds—17 Atlantics in all—against eight of the 4–6–0 type for express work. The two additional French compounds imported in 1905 were of the enlarged de Glehn type supplied to the Paris-Orleans Railway. These were similar to *La France*, but somewhat larger. The regular running of the French engines turn and turn about with the Swindon-built engines convinced Churchward that his own simple engines were at least the equal, if not the superior of the French compounds in efficiency, and much simpler to handle. But there was a feature of the French engines that much appealed to Churchward. The division of the drive between two axles enabled the rods and running gear to be made lighter, and a smoother-riding engine resulted. Consequently in 1906 he built an experimental four-cylinder simple Atlantic, for trial against the French compounds. This was the epoch-marking No. 40, later named the *North Star*.

This famous engine was intended solely for high-speed express passenger running and did not cut across the development of the two-cylinder " engine ", as exemplified in *Albion*, and which was being applied to a number of new types—4–4–0 passenger (" County " class), 2–8–0 heavy mineral, 2–6–2 heavy goods tank, and so on. In referring to this development special mention must be made of the valve gear, for which the Stephenson's link motion — inside — was standardised. Churchward's setting gave ideal performance for a general service locomotive, with high starting torque and efficient running at 50 to 60 m.p.h. In later years, with the Walschaerts valve gear coming into common use elsewhere outside the frames, Swindon's continued use of the inside gear was criticised on the grounds of inaccessibility, but actually there is sound reasoning behind the separation of valve gear and main driving rods. The occasions that a valve gear needs attention in a running shed are few compared to those when a big-end has to be taken down; and with the Swindon arrangement this latter job could be done without touching the valve gear.

This simple and desirable arrangement was of course not possible on a four-cylinder locomotive like the *North Star*. The French compounds had separate sets of Walschaerts gear on the high and low pressure cylinders, with those for the high pressure outside. Now Churchward, thoroughgoing realist though he was in so many ways, had one or two pet

crochets in design, which tried the ingenuity of his drawing office to the limit at times. One of these was an utter and complete embargo on outside valve gear, and a second was an insistence that cylinder centre lines must always be horizontal. The valve gear requirement led to the designing of a very neat, compact, and theoretically accurate motion for the four-cylinder engines. The arrangement used on the *North Star* was experimental, and usually referred to as the " scissors ", but on the " Star " class proper, introduced in 1907, he incorporated his clever, ingenious, but somewhat inaccessible version of the Walschaerts that was built into Swindon four-cylinder 4–6–0 locomotives over a period of more than 40 years. The *Dog Star*, illustrated on page , was indeed one of the great progenitors of British locomotive history.

Churchward was not prepared to stop at the " Stars ", tremendous advance though they represented over anything the GWR had possessed 10 years earlier. Traffic to and from the West of England was going up by leaps and bounds. Already the time was foreshadowed when something bigger than a 4–6–0 might be needed, and one recalls again his opening words in that classic paper; " the modern locomotive problem is principally a question of boiler ". So, in anticipation of what might be required before many years were out, he designed the largest boiler by far that had yet been seen in Great Britain. There was not yet the need for a complete *locomotive* of commensurately equivalent, so he took the " Star " layout of cylinders and machinery, lengthened the frames at the rear end to carry the enormous firebox, and put his huge experimental boiler on a 4–6–2 chassis. The result was the ever-memorable No. 111 *The Great Bear*. The nominal tractive effort was actually greater than that of the first " Stars ", because the cylinders were bored out to the maximum that castings from the patterns would permit. But this was only to the extent of increasing the diameter from $14\frac{1}{4}$ in. to 15 in. and increasing the tractive effort from 25,200 to 27,800 lb. " The Bear " was nevertheless an experiment in boilers, rather than a gigantic motive power unit. That it became a prestige symbol was, however, inevitable.

In the meantime production of the new standard range of locomotives was developing and older engines were receiving the new standard fully coned boilers. In due course the French compounds received them, and the " Aberdare " 2–6–0 goods, while the completion of Churchward's experiments with superheating, and development of the very effective form of top feed, introduced on either side of the safety valve bonnet completed the ultimate Swindon " look ", which was to remain standard and traditional for as long as locomotives of Great Western design were built in those works. Up till World War I all the locomotives were finished in what later became known as the " passenger " style, with copper-capped chimneys, polished brass safety valve bonnets, and fully lined out in the traditional Brunswick green livery. Churchward had simplified the earlier Dean style, by eliminating the red underframes and red wheels; but the engines of the 1906–1914 looked smart and ornate enough. All carried the company's coat of arms, either on the tender or the side tanks.

So far as the express passenger 4–6–0s were concerned it is clear that Churchward still regarded the two-cylinder type as the basic standard. They were cheaper to build than the four-cylinder, and while the latter were generally preferred for the long non-stop runs the two-cylinder variety definitely had the advantage on duties of an intermediate character, and where the climbing of heavy gradients were concerned. The construction programme at Swindon, from 1907 to 1914 was as follows:

Top: Pioneer of a large 4–4–0 class; No. 3312 *Bulldog* as originally built in 1899, with high raised Belpaire firebox. No other engine was built quite like this one, because it had a larger and higher-pitched boiler than the other domed engines of the period.

Middle: The second development of the " Bulldog " class, the " Camel " series of 1899, with curved frames, like *Bulldog* itself, but with domeless parallel boiler and high raised Belpaire firebox: engine No. 3352 *Camel.*

Year	Number built	
	2-cylinder	*4-cylinder*
1907	20	10
1908	—	10
1909	—	10
1910	—	7
1911	10	3
1912	10	—
1913	5	5
1914	—	15

So far as Churchward's own time was concerned, the development of the four-cylinder 4–6–0 reached finality in the " Princess " series of " Stars ", built in 1914. It had been found from much running experience that the steaming capacity of the boilers since superheating was such that the cylinder diameter could be increased to the maximum the castings would permit, and so the " Princesses " had 15 in. cylinders, making them equal in nominal tractive effort to *The Great Bear*.

A notable addition to the standard range of two-cylinder locomotives was the 2–6–0, of the 43XX series, introduced in 1911, which in due course became one of the most numerically strong of all Churchward designs. It was built extensively during the war years and a number of the class rendered excellent service for the Railway Operating Division of the British Army in France. It was during the war that the once-gay livery of Great Western locomotives was suppressed, and even the largest express passenger classes appeared in plain green. Safety valve covers were painted over and copper-capped chimneys were replaced by plain cast iron ones. The old traditional style was not restored until 1923, when the first of the " Castle " class was built.

Bottom: The 2–6–0 development of the ugly 4–6–0 No. 2601; engine No. 2602, first of the " Kruger " class heavy mineral engines, and forerunners of the " Aberdares ". The " Krugers " had 19 in. by 28 in. cylinders, 4 ft. 7½ in. coupled wheels and a boiler pressure of 180 lb. per sq. in.

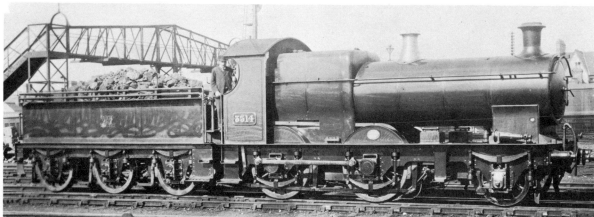

The domeless parallel boiler and Belpaire firebox applied to a variety of nineteenth century classes:—

Top left: No. 16 *Brunel*, of the " Armstrong " class.

Middle left: A small wheeled 2–4–0 of the 3501 class, the only one of its kind to receive a domeless boiler (1901); the latter was removed again in 1906.

Bottom left: One of the conversions from broad gauge tank engines of the 3521 class.

Above: A later example of the 3600 class 2–4–2 tank engine of 1900. The 31 engines of this class, built between 1900 and 1903, originally had the usual domeless parallel boiler of the period. This picture shows No. 3629 rebuilt with the coned boiler, later version of the Belpaire firebox, top feed, and superheater.

Below: A " Barnum " 2–4–0.

Top: A 7 ft. 8 in. Dean single, No. 3067 *Duchess of Teck*, entering Paddington. This engine received the domeless boiler and Belpaire firebox in 1902, but was rebuilt a second time with *domed* boiler in 1910. She was scrapped in 1914.

Above: The *Atbara* as originally built in 1900, showing the great height of the firebox above the line of the boiler, and the tender with the coal rails that were later replaced by raised side plates. The relatively narrow tapered chimney will also be noted.

Top: The celebrated 3440 *City of Truro* as built in 1903, and when her famous record run with the Ocean Mail was made in 1904. The difference between the tenders of these engines and those of the "Atbara" class will be noted.

Above: Pioneer engine of the "City" class as fitted with large copper capped chimney, and tender bearing the full name GREAT WESTERN and the company coat of arms, instead of the original inter-twined initials GWR. The *City of Bath* was later renumbered 3710.

Left: One of the later " Bulldogs " as originally built in 1904 with short cone taper boiler, narrow cast iron chimney, and straight frames, No. 3466 *Barbados.*

Below: One of the 157 class 2–2–2s, No. 165 with domeless boiler, at Paddington. This engine was the last GWR 2–2–2 to survive and was not scrapped until 1915.

Middle left: An " Atbara " in its final form, with long-cone taper boiler, top feed, and superheater. In this form the " Atbaras " formed part of the " Flower " class. No. 3379 *Kimberley* was later renumbered 4126 and was scrapped in 1927.

Bottom: The first GWR express passenger 4–6–0, No. 100, built in 1902. Named *Dean*, and then *William Dean*, and renumbered 2900, and fitted with standard taper boiler and superheater it became a member of the " Saint ", or 29XX class.

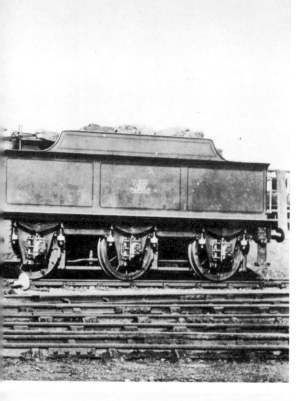

Top: The second GWR express passenger 4–6–0, No. 98, built in 1903, with the original short-cone taper boiler. This engine remained unnamed until 1907, when it was named *Vanguard*. It was renamed *Ernest Cunard* at the end of 1907 in honour of the latest elected director of the company. It was subsequently renumbered 2998.

Middle left: One of the Churchward Atlantics, similar to *Albion*; this engine, No. 179 *Magnet*, was built in April 1905 and rebuilt as a 4–6–0 in August 1912. At an early date it was renamed *Quentin Durward*, and after rebuilding as a 4–6–0 renumbered 2979.

Bottom left: Another of the Atlantic series named after characters in the Waverley Novels, No. 189 *Talisman*. It was rebuilt as a 4–6–0 in 1912 and subsequently renumbered 2989.

Bottom: First of the larger French compound Atlantics as originally delivered in 1905. It was then unnamed and had the plain chimney. This engine No. 103, here photographed at Bath, was subsequently named *President*.

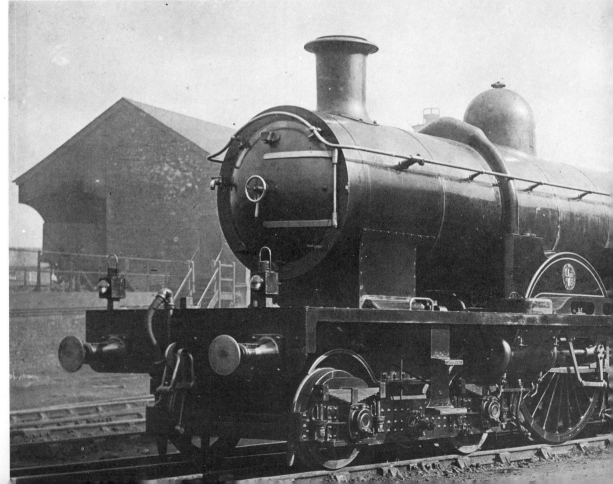

Above left: *North Star* as rebuilt in 1909 with a short cone superheated boiler and 4–6–0 wheel arrangement, but still retaining the original number 40. She was renumbered 4000 in 1912.

Above: *The* first GWR four-cylinder simple express locomotive No. 40, *North Star*, built in 1906 as an Atlantic. It is here seen photographed at Paddington, with the original square-stepped front framing.

Left: The first French compound Atlantic No. 102 *La France* as originally delivered, in 1903, and painted black, with the LNWR style of red and white lining, but carrying the GWR intertwined initials monogram on the centre panel of the tender.

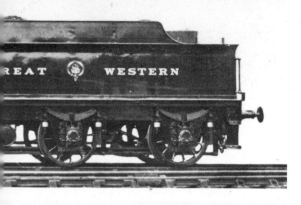

Top: One of the " Scott " series of two-cylinder express locomotives, built as an Atlantic but here seen as rebuilt in 1912 as a 4–6–0, with long-cone superheated boiler and top feed, but still retaining the original number, 183. This engine was later renumbered 2983, and the spelling of the name corrected from *Red Gauntlet* to *Redgauntlet*.

Middle: The first Great Western four-cylinder 4–6–0, No. 4001 *Dog Star*, built at Swindon, 1907, with long-cone taper boiler, non-superheated, and as yet not fitted with top feed.

Bottom: Churchward's giant Pacific of 1908, No. 111 *The Great Bear*, here seen in the final pre-war condition, with top feed added. This engine was superheated from the time of its construction.

Far bottom left: London district outer suburban train, carrying express passenger headlamps, passing Old Oak Common hauled by one of the " County Tanks ", No. 2223. These 4–4–2 engines worked as far as Oxford and Basingstoke on some duties.

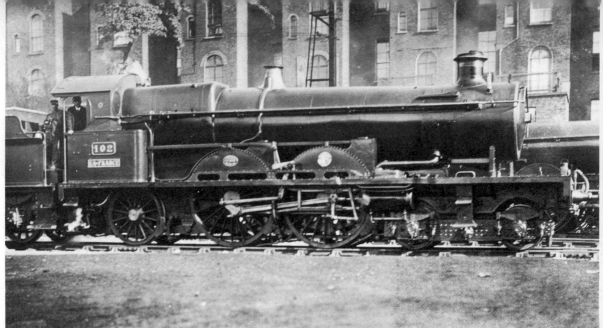

Above left: The first French compound No. 102 *La France* as rebuilt with the standard No. 1 superheated taper boiler. This engine was the last of the three de Glehn compounds to be rebuilt, this taking place in September 1916. It was then working from Oxford shed. *La France* was scrapped in 1926.

Above right: One of the later engines of the standard heavy mineral class of 2–8–0s, No. 2854, showing the beautiful condition in which these purely freight engines were maintained in days prior to World War I.

Below: A remarkable scene inside Old Oak Common sheds: the nearest engines, left to right, are No. 3393 *Auckland* (Atbara); 3071 *Emlyn;* 3809 *County Wexford;* 2915 *Saint Bartholomew.* Further 4–6–0 and " County " class engines can be seen in the background.

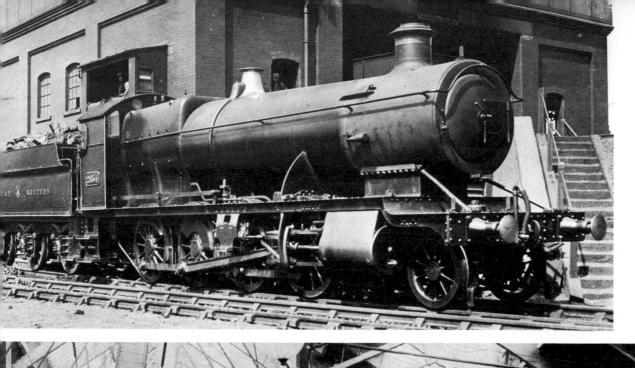

Above: The de Glehn compound No. 103 *President*, as reboilered a second time. It was first rebuilt with a non-superheated taper boiler, as fitted to the original series of " Stars " in February 1910 and received the superheated boiler, shown in this illustration in January 1914. This engine was scrapped in 1927.

Below left: The later style of the " County " class 4-4-0, with curved steps in the running plate, and superheated boiler with top feed. *County of Oxford* belongs to the final batch of 10 engines built in 1911–1912 Nos. 3821–3830, being the last of the entire class. The earlier ones, 3831–3839, and 3800–3820 were built in 1904–6.

Below right: One of the " Aberdare " 2-6-0s No. 2632, as rebuilt with taper boiler, superheater, and top feed. This photograph shows an unusual feature in the narrow tapered chimney fitted with a copper cap.

Top left: One of the highly successful 43XX class of 2–6–0s introduced in 1911, of which there were eventually no fewer than 322. The engine illustrated which is in such spanking condition, No. 4351, was built in 1914. The running numbers were 4300–4399; 5300–5399; 6300–6399; 7300–7321. Engines 6370–6399 and 7300–7304 were built by Robert Stephenson & Co. All the rest were built at Swindon.

Middle left: The final form of the two-cylinder express passenger 4–6–0, the "Court" series, with all the most modern features, and here seen in " photographic grey ". Though not the first of the series No. 2934 was chosen for the official photograph, probably because the owner of *Butleigh Court* (near Castle Cary) was a personal friend of Churchward.

Bottom left: One of the earlier two-cylinder 4–6–0s, built at Swindon in 1906, but as modernised and brought generally into line with the later standard

engine such as *Butleigh Court* (opposite). In this picture No. 2908 *Lady of Quality* has the later standard superheater boiler, with top feed, but retains the square step in the running plate, and the earlier arrangement of steps to the cab.

Top: One of the powerful 5 ft. 8 in. 2–8–0s built specially for the fast " fitted " night freight trains, No. 4702, built 1922, and photographed in Old Oak Common shed.

Above: The final variant of the " Star " class, one of the " Abbey " series of 1922, as originally built in plain green livery with tapered cast iron chimney; note also the hollow driving axles. This engine, No. 4063 *Bath Abbey*, stationed at Old Oak Common, has some outstanding performances to its credit.

Below: Up Worcester express in the cutting east of Twyford, worked by one of the Dean 7 ft. 8 in. singles in their final rebuilt condition with Belpaire firebox, " Atbara "-type cab, and top feed.

Bottom: Another pre-1914 photograph at Twyford showing an up South Wales express hauled by two-cylinder 4–6–0 No. 2952 *Twineham Court.* Except for the fourth coach, which is a " Concertina " 70-footer, the train is made up of 57 ft. " Toplight " stock, with a fine uniform appearance.

Part Four

At the Lineside

In the meantime, however, two notable new developments of the pure-Churchward era had taken place. There was first the 5 ft. 8 in. fast freight 2–8–0. The first of these had the standard No. 1 boiler, as on the 4–6–0 express engines, but then the larger and very handsome version was produced in 1921. This was an engine class with a limited utilisation—enough only to work the fast night " fitted " goods trains between London and Chester, London and Newton Abbot.

In 1922, after Churchward had retired, there came the final version of the " Star " class—twelve engines named after abbeys. They appeared in the plain green of wartime, with cast iron chimneys, but in two respects they were outstanding. They embodied the latest constructional techniques developed at Swindon during the war years, and were generally voted the best-ever among Great Western express locomotives of the day. An important detail improvement was the use of hollow driving axles, which permitted of more uniform and precise metallurgical treatment of the steel, and also, by way of a bonus gave a slight reduction in weight. Any photographer who had freedom to roam the Great Western in the last twenty years before grouping would have reaped an incredibly rich reward in the tremendous variety of locomotives and coaching stock then in service. Times of transition are always interesting, but never more so than when a positive revolution is in progress, as certainly it was in the years 1902 to 1914. It was a revolution in almost every aspect of running the trains. The opening of the various new and shortened main lines was being followed by complete revision of the timetables. The principal West of England expresses were running via Westbury; from 1910 there were two-hour expresses from Paddington to Birmingham, via Bicester, while there was a new express service from Wolverhampton and Birmingham to the West of England, via Stratford-on-Avon. The photographs included in the first three sections of this book show something of the variety that accompanied the evolution of narrow-gauge locomotive design, while the carriages were in no less striking a metamorphosis. To crown all these were changing liveries, both of locomotives and carriages. Many relics of the broad gauge were to be seen in the sidings of West Country stations, where the " baulk road " remained.

There were not all that many expert railway photographers at work during this exciting period, particularly those who could secure a good picture of a fast train in motion. Fortunately, however, Dr. T. F. Budden, and Mr. H. Gordon Tidey travelled about considerably, while in the London area F. E. Mackay's superb documentaries have recorded the early days of the new Churchward locomotives. In this section the captions to individual photographs tell the story as clearly as any description can do, and they have been arranged as a miscellany, rather than in any precise geographical or chronological sequence. It has not been possible to pin-point all the locations in this fascinating series of pictures, nor in all cases the individual locomotives. In date they range from the last years of the broad gauge, when the mixed gauge was still in use through Bath and on the Bristol and Exeter main line, to the years just before the grouping, when the new " Abbey " class 4–6–0s were hauling such loads that in a photograph on straight track the tail end of the train was too far away for the exact number of coaches to be counted.

The pictures form an epitome of Great Western history in other ways, as when there was a through passenger train service between Southall and Victoria (London Chatham & Dover) station; when the South Devon line along the coast between Dawlish and Teignmouth was still single line, and when the " Cornish Riviera Express ", as first introduced and running via Bristol, was made up mostly of clerestory-roofed carriages. Although the temporary abandonment of the old chocolate-and-cream coach livery was regretted by the sentimentalists, there was something very dignified about the crimson lake that superseded it, especially in a completely uniform rake of the new elliptical-roofed stock, with every carriage having its scarlet roof board. Just imagine spending a day at the lineside in the cutting east of Twyford, around 1911 or 1912! " Saints ", " Stars " and the occasional Atlantic on the heaviest trains; " Cities ", " Atbaras " and " Counties " on some of the Worcesters, not forgetting the occasional Dean single, and the changing of engines at Reading on some trains for the Weymouth line, which might have a domeless boilered " Barnum " down from Paddington, and a " Bulldog " from there onwards. The last of the 2–2–2 singles remained at Oxford until 1915, but these did not come often to Reading at that time.

Then there was the variety of tank engines. The new 4–4–2s came high-stepping along, very impressive with their big wheels and their lengthy piston stroke; but the smaller inside-cylindered 2–4–2s were also in evidence nipping along, with express headlamps, on the Oxford semi-fasts, which always seemed to leave Paddington with more coaches in

80

successive slip portions than in the main part of the train. The favourite spots for photography around London were Old Oak Common and Acton (F. E. Mackay) with the occasional excursion to Park Royal on the short route to Birmingham. Gordon Tidey frequented Twyford, while Dr. Budden seems to have made Acton and Ealing Broadway his centres of operation. But Dr. Budden also spent a good deal of time around Bath, and made the most of his opportunities, with " bags " extending from the " *volte-face* 0–4–4 to 4–4–0 " 35XX class to *The Great Bear*.

These photographs of trains at speed are as interesting from the coaching stock point of view as for the locomotives. It was in 1904 that new construction of the traditional clerestory-roofed stock ended and the first of the revolutionary " Dreadnoughts " appeared. These were introduced first as dining cars on to the inaugural " Cornish Riviera " rake in 1904, which otherwise consisted entirely of clerestory-roofed Dean corridor stock. But the introduction a year later of the full " Dreadnought " sets on to the " Cornish Riviera Express " was anything but popular with passengers, however impressive the new coaches might have looked externally. We have a picture of the all-" Dreadnought " " Cornish Riviera " photographed near Wellington (Somerset) and hauled by an Atlantic. The feature of the " Dreadnoughts " that caused their great unpopularity was the entrances only at the ends, and in the centres. There is a further picture of a complete train of these coaches on a two-hour Birmingham-London express.

The " Concertinas " followed. These were splendid 70 ft. vehicles in which the individual doors for each compartment were restored, but like the " Dreadnoughts " built so wide that the doors had to be set back slightly so that the handles did not extend beyond the profile. The 70 ft. coaches were limited in their route availability, being restricted generally to the West of England, South Wales and Birmingham route. It was to provide modern elliptical-roofed stock for the important North to West services that the 57 ft.

"Toplight" stock was introduced in 1907. The term "toplight" arose from the provision of frosted glass windows above the ordinary windows. The "Dreadnoughts" and the "Concertinas" also had these top lights, but had the other nicknames to distinguish them. It was in 1908 that the historic chocolate and cream livery was discontinued. For a short time coaches were painted a medium brown, and there was an F. Moore colour plate of the "Cornish Riviera Express" with a seven-coach set of "Dreadnought" coaches in this interim style hauled by the 4–6–0 engine *Knight of the Grand Cross*. The crimson-lake livery was very fine, plentifully lined out, and on express trains always set off by the scarlet roofboards that gave such comprehensive information as:

1. PENZANCE, PLYMOUTH, BRISTOL, STRATFORD-ON-AVON, BIRMINGHAM & WOLVERHAMPTON.
2. PADDINGTON, BIRMINGHAM, SHREWSBURY, CHESTER & BIRKENHEAD.
3. PLYMOUTH, BRISTOL, SHREWSBURY, CREWE, CARLISLE & GLASGOW CENTRAL.

It was in the early 1900s that the vogue of the steam rail motor car developed in Great Britain, from combined carriage and engine designed by Dugald Drummond for the joint use of the London & South Western, and the London Brighton & South Coast Railways between Fratton and Havant. The GWR borrowed one of these vehicles for a short time in 1903, and from this Churchward designed his own cars. The motive power was provided by a pair of horizontal outside cylinders, supplied from a vertical boiler enclosed within the carriage body. An interesting feature was the use of the Walschaerts valve gear outside, doubtless because any form of inside valve gear would have been quite inaccessible beneath the floor of the carriage. These little units became so popular that by the end of 1908 the GWR had no fewer than 99 of its own design in operation, many of them hauling trailers. They were employed on the shorter branch lines, as "between-time", off-peak services, and had a lengthy lease of life. As a schoolboy I used to travel daily on one that left Reading at 3.45 p.m. and ran to Basingstoke, calling at Mortimer and Bramley en route.

In later years I became very familiar with another that ran the Chippenham and Calne branch. This unit had a wider scope. In the 1920s two of the afternoon West of England expresses still ran via Bristol and both detached a slip coach at Chippenham. With some ingenuity this coach was used to provide a through service from Paddington to wayside stations between Chippenham and Bath, and was worked forward from Chippenham as trailer to one of the rail motor cars. This gave quite an excellent service from London to stations like Corsham, Box and Bathampton. The disadvantage of a rail motor car as such was, of course, that if the "engine" had to be withdrawn for maintenance or repairs, the whole car was out of action. Later practice was to have one or two trailers coupled, for push-and-pull working, to a small tank locomotive of standard design.

A further group of photographs show something of the fascinating scene in the West Country during the early 1900s. The junction at Brent, the animated scene at Truro station, and the view of the Royal Albert Bridge, with track still laid on the "baulk road" have a period flavour that plain words can scarcely convey. It is interesting to recall that the broad-gauge line across the Tamar was part of the section included in the historic weekend programme in May, 1892 when the final conversion of the gauge was carried out at such speed. From these I come to a final contrast in West of England express train workings, as illustrating what Churchward was providing for when he began his classic locomotive development in the late 1890s. There is first of all the 19th century train, hauled by a Dean single, in all its elegance; then a West of England express just after the introduction of the "Concertina" stock—and then finally the "Cornish Riviera Express" of 1922.

Above left: A remarkable shot on Goring water troughs showing an up express hauled by the " Armstrong " class 4–4–0 No. 16 *Brunel*, rebuilt with parallel domeless boiler. The cloud of spray from an overflowing tender was a most unusual sight on the GWR, though common enough at one time on the LNWR.

Left: One of the last batch of " Counties ", with curved steps on the running plate working an up two-hour Birmingham express composed entirely of " Dreadnought " stock, painted in the crimson-lake livery. The set is unusual in that it carries no roof-boards. The photograph was taken near Ruislip.

Right: An interesting two-train picture at Southall. On the left is a close-coupled train of four-wheeled stock leaving for Victoria, while on the down main line a " County " class 4–4–0 is approaching with a West of England express via Bristol including " Concertina " and clerestory stock.

Below: West of England express ready to leave Paddington. The engine, No. 2905 *Lady Macbeth* is in the original condition, non-superheated. This photograph shows well, from the rear, the curving shape of Churchward's form of the Belpaire firebox. The leading coach is one of the new elliptical roof types, while the chocolate and cream livery still persisted.

Above: Another interesting scene near Acton in early narrow gauge days. The up express, hauled by one of the " Camel " series of 4–4–0s, No. 3353 *Blasius*, has a typical mixed rake of milk vans, horse boxes, and some distinctly ancient clerestory coaches.

Below: _La France_ on one of her final duties. When Stationed at Oxford the French compounds were frequently on the Bournemouth-Newcastle through express, between Basingstoke and Banbury. At one time GWR engines had certain turns forward from Banbury to Leicester over the Great Central line. In this photograph taken near Cholsey the train is composed of GCR stock.

Middle right: Early narrow gauge days in the London area. A " Badminton " class 4–4–0, No. 3304 *Oxford*, is seen in original condition on a Birmingham and North express between Old Oak Common and Acton. The train is composed entirely of clerestory coaches.

Bottom right: A heavy down West of England express passing Old Oak Common hauled by two 7 ft. 8 in. Dean single wheelers. The leading engine is No. 3076 *Princess Beatrice;* the train engine is unidentified. Note the fine bracket signals of the type that remained standard for upwards of 40 years.

Top: An easy task for *Albion* in her original condition. This photograph must have been taken in the first year of her existence 1903–4, before her temporary conversion to the 4–4–2 type. The leading vehicle in this light train is one of the bogie brake and luggage vans, an earlier version of which was included in the first all-corridor train of 1892.

Middle: An interesting example of a combined medium-distance express train, with several slip portions, running near Acton. The main part of the train is a four-coach clerestory set, complete with roof-boards, to which five additional coaches are attached in rear. The engine is one of the 36XX class of 2–4–2 tanks, rebuilt with superheater, taper boiler, and top feed, No. 3601.

Bottom: The " Cornish Riviera Express " near Wellington (Somerset) with a five-coach set of "Dreadnought " stock in chocolate and cream livery. The engine is an Atlantic, No. 172 *The Abbot*, with short-cone taper boiler. This engine was not converted to a 4–6–0 until 1912.

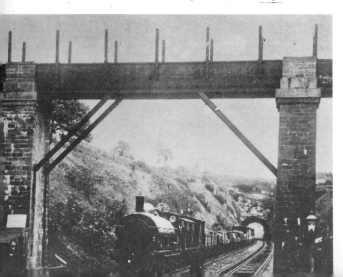

Top: One of the new 2–6–2 tank engines of 1906, as originally built, with a heavy coal train on the main line in South Wales. These engines were designed in the first place for freight service, but were later developed into the standard type for heavy passenger suburban work.

Above: One of the earliest Birmingham-Paddington expresses, by the new route opened in 1910, running near Park Royal. The photograph shows the leading coach still in the chocolate and cream livery, but the engine, No. 2902 *Lady of the Lake* has been rebuilt with superheater, and top feed

added. The light formation was typical of the trains running on the new route in its early days.

Above right: Royal occasion in March 1902, when King Edward VII and Queen Alexandra visited the West Country. After the Royal Train had been run non-stop from Paddington to Kingswear the journey was continued to Plymouth, and the train was worked from Newton Abbot onwards by " Bulldog " class 4–4–0 No. 3357 originally named *Exeter,* but renamed *Royal Sovereign* specially for the occasion. The train is seen here on arrival at Plymouth, with the engine standing on " baulk road ".

Below right: The " Cornish Riviera Express " in 1904, with the original six-coach rake, clerestory, except for the " Dreadnought " dining car. The engine is the pioneer GWR express passenger 4–6–0 No. 100 *William Dean* in original condition, with parallel domeless boiler, while the line on the sea wall between Dawlish and Teignmouth was then single-tracked. The train is at the west end of Parsons Tunnel.

Left: The makings of a mystery at Flax Bourton, in the final broad gauge days. A down narrow-gauge goods train hauled by one of the saddle tank engines is standing on the up line. This may have been a case of " wrong-line working " during a civil engineer's possession; but it could have been the temporary shunting of the goods on to the up line to clear the way for a down express passenger train.

Above: An " Ocean Mail " special leaving Fishguard Harbour. This was the occasion of the first call of the Cunard liner *Mauretania*, on August 30, 1909. The " Atbara " class 4–4–0 No. 3381 *Maine* took the all-mail three-coach special as shown in this illustration and was followed by two passenger specials, each hauled by two 4–4–0 engines.

Top right: One of the " Aberdare " class insidecylinder 2–6–0s working a heavy mixed goods westwards near Oldfield Park, Bath. The engine is fitted with taper boiler but without superheater and top feed.

Middle left: North to West express, via the Severn Tunnel, leaving Shrewsbury, including GW and LNW stock. The leading engine is an unidentified " Atbara ", while the train engine shows the very unusual use on this route of a Dean 7 ft. 8 in. single. In the background, partly obscured by smoke from the leading engine, are the Coleham sheds of the LNWR, while in the foreground is an LNWR saddle tank 0–6–0.

Bottom left: The pioneer GWR 4–6–0 express passenger engine, No. 100 *William Dean*, as modified by the fitting of a short cone taper boiler, here seen working a local stopping train near Bathampton. Then, as in later years, these stopping trains were used as running-in turns for express passenger engines newly built, or repaired at Swindon Works.

Left: A picture of outstanding interest taken prior to the abolition of the broad gauge at the point where the line passes through Sidney Gardens, Bath. The local train is composed of very ancient narrow-gauge stock and is hauled by a 2–2–2 engine of the " Sir Alexander " class.

Top: The variety of locomotives to be seen around Bath: a highly polished 0–4–2 tank working a local train near Bathampton. The width of the formation shows clearly the recent conversion from the broad gauge.

Above: This interesting shot of *The Great Bear*, near Bathampton, on an up West of England express reveals the immediate post-war period, when No. 111 had a tapered cast iron chimney instead of the original copper-capped one. Though not definitely identified the train is probably the 2.10 p.m. up from Bath, non-stop to Paddington.

Top right: A local train from the Avon valley line approaching the junction at Bathampton, with a train mostly of old four-wheeled stock. The engine is one of the 3521 class rebuilds which originated as broad gauge 0–4–2 tanks and were later rebuilt from 0–4–4 narrow gauge tank engines into 4–4–0s.

Middle right: One of the numerous steam rail motor cars, hauling a non-corridor clerestory coach, and here seen on the Chippenham to Calne branch.

Bottom right: Period piece in South Devon: a down goods, double-headed by a standard Dean 0–6–0 and a saddle tank 0–6–0 rounding the curve into Brent station. The branch line to Kingsbridge is seen falling away on the right. Note the highly burnished condition of both these goods engines.

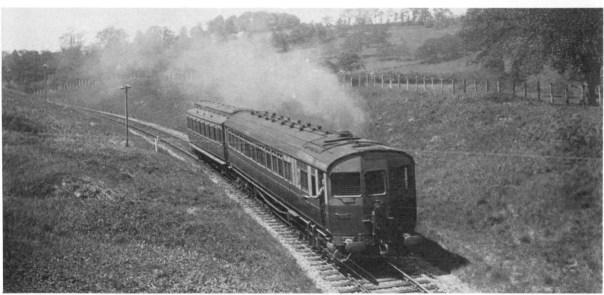

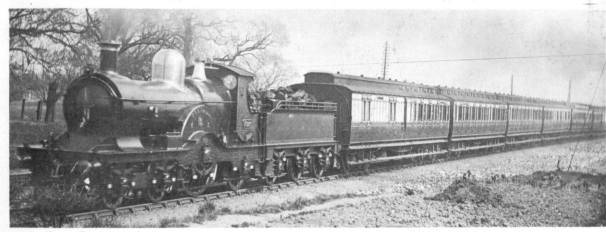

Below: Brent junction viewed from the overbridge, with a local passenger train, tank engine-hauled, approaching the station on the down main line, while a goods is standing in the siding on the down side. The steeply falling gradient of the Kingsbridge branch is apparent in this photograph.

Top left: A veteran 4–4–0 tank engine on the Liskeard and Looe branch. Originally a 2–4–2 well tank built in 1886, it was rebuilt in 1897, and at first worked on the Highworth branch from Swindon. As shown in this illustration it had 16 in. by 21 in. cylinders, 4 ft. 1 in. coupled wheels, and a boiler pressure of 140 lb. per sq. in. Scrapped 1926. The beautiful turn-out was no more than typical of all Great Western locomotives prior to 1914.

Middle left: Main line evolution—I: a West of England express just after the conversion of the gauge, with Dean corridor coaches, restaurant car (fifth from engine) and hauled by Dean 7 ft. 8 in. single No. 3026 *Tornado*. The location is immediately west of Old Oak Common.

Bottom left: : Truro station, down side: at left, a branch train headed by one of the 3521 class small-wheeled rebuilt 4–4–0s; on the main line is a train for Penzance headed by " Bulldog " class 4–4–0 No. 3432 *River Yealm*. The Falmouth branch train is in the bay on extreme right.

Bottom right: A fine view of the Royal Albert Bridge from Saltash station. The track is still laid on the longitudinal " baulk road " of Brunel. The engine of the approaching train is a " Duke " class 4–4–0, the standard passenger type in Cornwall in the first years after the abolition of the broad gauge.

Top: **Main line evolution—II**: a West of England express composed mainly of "Concertina" stock, in chocolate and cream, with "Dreadnought" dining car (sixth from engine) and clerestory coaches in rear. The engine is No. 4005 *Polar Star*, which in 1910 participated in the interchange trials with the LNWR.

Above: **Main line evolution—III**: the "Cornish Riviera Express" in 1922, with *at least* "fourteen on", passing Twyford, and hauled by one of the latest four-cylinder 4–6–0s No. 4065 *Evesham Abbey* in plain green, though the chocolate and cream livery has been restored on the coaching stock.